# APPALACHIAN
## R E V I E W

**VOL. 48, NO. 2**
**SPRING 2020**

**TRADITION. DIVERSITY. CHANGE.**

# EDITOR
Jason Kyle Howard

## BOOK REVIEWS EDITOR
Emily Masters

## STUDENT ASSISTANTS
Frankie Baldwin, Skylar Bensheimer,
& Rhea Carter

## MANUSCRIPT READERS
Katherine Scott Crawford & Patti Frye Meredith

ESTABLISHED IN 1973
PUBLISHED QUARTERLY
by Berea College
CPO 2166
205 N. Main Street
Berea, Kentucky 40404
www.appalachianreview.net

The short stories in this publication are works of fiction. Names, characters, places, and incidents are either the products of the authors' imaginations or are used fictitiously. Any resemblance to actual events, locales, or persons, living or dead, is entirely coincidental. The views expressed in the creative nonfiction herein are solely those of the authors.

Electronic submissions only at www.appalachianreview.net

Distributed by the University of North Carolina Press. Basic subscription price: $30/year for individuals, $40/year for institutions. For subscription requests and inquiries, visit the magazine's website, email uncpress_journals@unc.edu, or call 919.962.4201.

# CONTENTS

EDITOR'S NOTE........................*Jason Kyle Howard*    6

**2019 DENNY C. PLATTNER AWARDS**...........................    9

**FICTION**

Bethany Holmstrom

    *Pile of Feathers*........................................................    11

Mary Alice Hostetter

    *Traps*.......................................................................    79

Vanessa Van Besien

    *Milk*.......................................................................    102

**CREATIVE NONFICTION**

Rebecca Hazelwood

    *Secondhand Stories*................................................    38

**POETRY**

Frank X Walker

    *On Mother's Day*....................................................    28

    *Hairline Fracture*...................................................    30

    *DeeJay Battle*.........................................................    31

    *Y'all Say I Do, We Say Black Lives Matter*...........    33

    *Mrs. Butterworth, Uncle Ben, & Aunt Jemima*.......    34

    *Baptism by Dirt*.....................................................    35

    *Commencement 2020*.............................................    36

Jenn Blair

    *Beersheba Springs Assembly* .......................................... 52

    *After the Prodigal Returned* ........................................ 54

    *Hellbender* ................................................................ 56

    *The Flood* ................................................................. 57

    *Paper* ...................................................................... 58

L. Renée

    *Gone* ........................................................................ 72

    *Fish Fry* .................................................................... 76

Jae Dyche

    *On Birds* ................................................................... 96

    *Elegy as a Railroad Watch* ......................................... 98

    *Axis Mundi* .............................................................. 101

Lisa M. Kendrick

    *Match Girl* ............................................................... 116

    *Jawbreaker* ............................................................... 117

Alison Terjek

    *Leaving the Mountains* ............................................... 118

Elizabeth Gordon

    *Almost Heaven, or Mixed-Race Road Trip Following*

    *the Fall of Saigon* ..................................................... 136

**INTERVIEW**

Robert Gipe

    *Carter Sickels* .......................................................... 60

**BOOK REVIEWS**

Savannah Sipple

    *The Book of Daniel* by Aaron Smith ................................. 119

Emily Masters

    *Appalachia North* by Matthew Ferrence ......................... 123

Donna M. Crow

    *The Ash Family* by Molly Dektar .................................... 125

Sylvia Woods
    *Planted By the Signs* by Misty Skaggs .................................     129
Melissa Helton
    *LGBTQ Fiction and Poetry from Appalachia* (Jeff Mann
    & Julia Watts, eds.) ..............................................................     133

**CONTRIBUTORS** .......................................................     139

**COVER PHOTOGRAPH**
*Justice Undone—Untitled #14* by Raymond Thompson Jr.

# EDITOR'S NOTE

JASON KYLE HOWARD

W hen *Appalachian Heritage* was founded in 1973 by the poet Albert Stewart, it offered a haven for regional writers whose work had often been overlooked and dismissed by literary gatekeepers. Twelve years later, the publication found a permanent home at Berea College in a partnership that fused Stewart's welcoming vision with the mission of abolitionist John G. Fee, who founded the institution in 1855 as the first integrated, coeducational college in the South on the principle that "God has made of one blood all peoples of the earth."

Over the past few years we have increasingly noticed that our name has sparked confusion for some who assume that as a publication containing the word "heritage," we somehow stand for, at best, a simplistic view of Appalachia as a place frozen in a quaint, bucolic, homogenous past or, at worst, a particular ultra-conservative brand of politics and identity. In response to our social media posts, including some promoting work we have published by writers of color and members of the LGBTQ+ community, we have seen an alarming increase in comments that are derogatory, racist, xenophobic, homophobic, transphobic, and misogynist in nature.

While we have been having conversations about a new name over the last couple of years, now seems like a good time to make this statement. In recent weeks, from coast to coast and across the Appalachian region, we have witnessed extraordinary, moving, and necessary demonstrations of protest and outrage directed at police brutality and systemic racism. We as a publication stand on the side of justice and in solidarity with our parent institution's founding principle of equality and support for marginalized communities.

Assumptions about our name are in stark contrast not only to our core values as a publication, but also to the diverse identities and complexities of Appalachia we strive to highlight. It has raised the question of how we might honor our publication's history and founding while remaining true to the progressive principles we have long held dear.

Following a year of consultations with Berea College administration and informal conversations with some of the region's writers, we are announcing that from this issue forward we will be known as *Appalachian Review*. This transition will allow us to maintain our Appalachian orientation as intended by our founding editor while also making clear our vision as a contemporary literary magazine: to "showcase the work of emerging and established writers throughout Appalachia and beyond, offering readers literature that is thoughtful, innovative, and revelatory."

We will always honor our magazine's founder, Albert Stewart, and teach others about his important contributions to the study and literature of our region. In moving forward we also plan to adopt the motto of the Berea College Loyal Jones Appalachian Center: *Tradition. Diversity. Change.* This addition will serve as a reminder of our history and the values reflected in our mission, as well as linking us more closely to the LJAC itself.

We want to be crystal clear in our values. We celebrate an Appalachia that is inclusive and welcoming—where Black lives matter, where the LGBTQ+ community, people of color, and immigrants have a place at the literary table. We want to publish even more work reflecting those voices and experiences, which have always been integral to Appalachia, and to remember that we are, indeed, one blood. ■

# 2019 DENNY C. PLATTNER AWARDS

The annual Plattner Awards were established in 1995 by Kenneth and Elissa Plattner to honor their late son and his love of writing. The awards are given to the finest pieces of fiction, creative nonfiction, and poetry that appeared in *Appalachian Review* during the previous year. Winners receive a $200 prize, and both winners and honorable mentions are awarded a handsome cherry wooden book rack designed and manufactured by Berea College Crafts.

## FICTION
*Judged by Leah Hampton, author of*
F*ckface: And Other Stories

Winner: Kathryn Milam, "Smart House"
Honorable Mention: Davis Enloe, "Earth, Sky, Trees"

## CREATIVE NONFICTION
*Judged by Jake Maynard, noted essayist, editor, and teacher*

Winner: Catharina Coenen, "Invasive"
Honorable Mention: Larry Bingham, "What My Father Heard"

## POETRY
*Judged by Savannah Sipple, author of*
WWJD and Other Poems

Winner: Jane Sasser, "Chiaroscuro"
Honorable Mention: Summar West, "Almanac"

# PILE OF
# FEATHERS

BETHANY HOLMSTROM

The pile of feathers was right in the middle of the dirt side-path, leading to the ruins of a tobacco shed. The feathers were clean, June noticed that first: as if freshly plucked, no hint of parasites or smell of decay.

"Get away, Elvis." The hound dog abandoned his tentative approach at her command; then, nose in air, he bayed and bounded up the ridge. The portly chocolate lab Riley followed, barreling recklessly from the gravel road and through the stickers of the wineberry patch.

She took her thin aluminum hiking pole, the metallic teal poking into the black and brown and white heap, widening its diameter. No markings to give the species away: and no flesh, only ivory bones at the base, the downy assemblage hiding the ossified parts below. Not a small creature, but hardly a hawk or eagle either.

A faint growl of thunder came from the gathering clouds on the far end of the valley; with the vagaries of summer storms, she might not have much time summit and return. The pile bothered June, hiking as quickly as her knees allowed—all the way up to the bald at McFalls mountain where the Starkeys used to bring their cattle to graze each season, and then down the back way, along the steep, abandoned logging road.

■ ■ ■

One May, eight or so years ago, a headless bird appeared in her yard. But that bird was intact otherwise, its inky-black feathers and red talons undisturbed. One wing sprawled out, the other tucked under, as if in its natural state of rest. Nothing to suggest the guillotine.

The dogs performed disinterest. She walked the perimeter of the yard proper, defined by the creek and the gravel road to the north, the woods sloping up to the ridge on the southern side, the park mountains to the west, McFalls Mountain to the east. No other disturbances.

She buried the corpse under a dogwood by the driveway— only a foot down, but hoping the proximity to the house would be enough to deter the coyotes.

Two weeks later, when she came back from picking up the tomato plants they had on hold for her at the nursery in town: carnage. Nineteen headless fowl of varying sizes strewn about the lawn. But—she could tell this time—all chickens. Like some elaborate and devastating mass ritual had been conducted.

■ ■ ■

George Young did not bear the loss of his poultry easily.

"I catch them dogs on my land 'gain, I'm gonna shoot 'em. No more pot shots. That one, the big brown one, I tried to get him in the rear this time at least, but I ain't gon' be so forgivin' next time. That there's a monster." Riley gently snored from his orthopedic bed, back leg twitching—most likely dreaming of the melee. "All twenty-three of my chickens, those dogs killed. Dug right under the fencin'."

She could imagine George Young: overalls and old white t-shirt, pits stained, hems frayed, work boots and ball cap, standing in his kitchen with its pine wood panelling and yellowed linoleum, chain-smoking as he spoke into the mint green phone hanging on the wall, resolutely staring at his gun rack by the tattered blue recliner in the living room.

"Do you remember, Mr. Young, when we used to come and visit, when Mark was little?"

A confused pause: a slight sense of a trap. "Sure. Always knew when y'all were comin', on account of the party line with your folks."

"Indeed. Your wife always brought us the best apple butter."

"Yes, well. She was always one for spoilin' children."

"Yes. And I don't know if you recall the time she was out of town, and we invited everyone for Mark's fourth birthday party, and your horse wandered on over and up and died in my parents' vegetable garden, right before the cake..."

A strategic break, to conjure forth the screams and the sobs over the uneaten cake of the traumatized birthday boy. Mr. Young had heard them, when he hurried from the next ridge over; Mark snuck out of the house and began anew, as the adults encircled the dead horse's body amidst the zucchini and considered their next steps.

"No accounting for animal behavior, really," June reminded him.

"Yes, well...suppose that's the case, yes." Mr. Young's combative tone diminished, sunk lower by his defeat: guilted by this Yankee-fied snob, who didn't even move back home to take care of her parents properly, when they aged and sickened. June just tucked them away in a home. And then, only a few months before her parents died, one after the other, she came waltzing back down with her teenage son, and all her plans to update and fix the homestead. Her accent polished away with all that book money.

They settled on a number to pay back Mr. Young for the chickens, and June got a contractor out to fix the coop within the week.

■ ■ ■

"Are you *suuure* it wasn't another chicken, Mom?"

"It was *not* a chicken," June snapped, wondering why she had told him about the hike.

Even over the phone, she heard the edges of his smile. The chicken massacre story and its aftermath was a favorite of Mark's—he probably embellished on it at dinner parties in the city, at friends' and colleagues' houses up the Hudson Valley, by crackling fireplaces after a day of skiing in Vermont. Telling them what it was like to live a real country life. Pausing as his audience laughed incredulously at the image of the decapitated chickens and fallen horse among the squash, to sip his single malt—rolling the peat and smoke around his tongue, tasting what it meant to move rich people's money around, and make them richer.

But who was June to judge; she had sold out in her own right, eventually tiring of her fraught creation that made her so financially comfortable. Ghost writers at her publisher now churned out the latest best-selling crimes to be puzzled out by the New Orleans lady detective June gave life to thirty years ago.

"Well," Mark said, "if the remains are still there when we go for a hike, you can show us." His tone was placating, almost patronizing.

Us. June did not begrudge her son his second wedding— not the bloated budget, nor the awkward politeness involved

*They knew each other's movements from afar, dutifully charting and plotting out their existences in their weekly Sunday phone calls.*

at the event, sitting yet again with her ex and his husband at the shared "family" table, making small talk with Mark's father: as if they shared anything beyond the formation of a zygote and a few horribly inadequate years together. But June didn't entirely understand the second marriage, either; she simply couldn't grasp the compulsion to try again. The naive optimism that propelled her son entirely eluded her. Mark's first marriage to his college sweetheart ended abruptly after five years. June never received the particulars on that beyond "we outgrew each other"—but then her relationship with her son was politely antiseptic. They knew each other's movements from afar, dutifully charting and plotting out their existences in their weekly Sunday phone calls.

"Remember the train gets in late on Thursday, you sure it's not too late?" As if she hadn't put it on her wall calendar two months ago: "Mark + Kate 10pm Train / Crescent." And then, a few days later, "Mark + Kate 10am."

"Yes, I'm still perfectly capable of driving at night."

A sigh. "That's not what I meant, Mom."

What he meant was he felt how the air tingled and tensed when other people came into June's valley. That he knew about the sacrosanct ways in which she wrangled her hours—routines born from decades of solitude. How dishes were washed every night, since there was no excuse when typically only one place setting was involved. A cloth napkin was used for precisely two days, unless an egregiously saucy dinner disrupted the schedule. The temperature of the bedrooms upstairs at night, the way towels were folded, the chairs that were used more often than others: Mark saw how the materials and spaces of her life were curated. How after three days—even with her closest friends and increasingly infrequent lovers—the maxim about guests and fish prevailed. Mark had only the tiniest taste of what that meant, to cultivate a life alone: but he knew enough to sense the limits of his mother's hospitality, and how she failed to acknowledge them in turn.

"I'll be there at ten," June told him.

■ ■ ■

When the good city of Lynchburg renovated the train station in conjunction with the commuter rail service, they decided the narrow cobblestone street that precipitously dropped into the tiny, eight-car parking lot below, down by the tracks, was too difficult and too quaint to alter: and so, as the trains come and go, one can hear the angry jostling of rolling luggage and the sometimes rancorous cries out of rolled down windows as cars attempted to execute six plus point turns in the confined space and work their way back up the slope.

"Just park at the top by the far set of stairs," Mark had texted her. "It's easier."

And she saw him, her boy, from her station wagon at other end of the station, as he instructed: first the carefully groomed salt-and-pepper hair, then the build with the slightest suggestion of the tended-to musculature below, the inoffensively charming features—except why, oh why, did he have his father's lack of chin definition. Mark was carrying both their matching bags, and Kate followed shortly after; yoga-toned, a wisp of a thing, with long thick dark hair that fell in perfect layers, the lightest of makeup, a cashmere cardigan draped over her shoulders for the over-air conditioned train car—all softness and roses and cedar as she hugged her mother-in-law. Kate sat in the passenger seat, Mark in the back.

On the forty-minute drive to June's house, they spoke of the train ride down: the children who didn't stop crying, the people who didn't wear headphones, the over-priced beer in the cafe car. Then June heard all about the couple's recent trip to Sonoma and the impending renovations to the brownstone they just closed on in Park Slope. It was Kate's first time down to visit, and so she commented on the darkness, the solitude, the way no other cars appeared, the lack of demarcation on the paved road.

The dogs somehow knew—sensed the additional presences in the car as it rolled down the hill into the valley. Mark returned their exuberance; Kate winced as her husband sank down into the soft summer lawn, the mud and clay gathering on the knees of his jeans as he buried his face into the fur and tongues and slobber offered up to him.

■ ■ ■

Early Saturday morning, before the heat and humidity could smother their resolve, they prepared to hike up McFalls.

"It's so relaxing here," Kate sighed as she watched the ruby-throated hummingbirds dart and joust each other around the feeder hanging off the side porch, waiting for Mark to finish coating himself in all-natural insect repellant. June found Kate's incessant wonder slightly irritating, by this point. How Kate found it freeing there was no cell phone service and only the barest of Wi-Fi. How Kate thought it was charming that you had to walk a half mile down the private gravel road to get the paper and the mail. How Kate was certain that the untrained orchestra of crickets and tree frogs at night was better than any sound machine you could buy.

As they hiked and the tobacco shed was about to become visible around the next bend, June realized she had no intention of bringing up the odd feathers. Not after Mark's teasing on the phone call. She hoped he'd forgotten.

"Hey Mom, wasn't that bird's body around here somewhere?"

The pile was still there, almost exactly as she had left it; there was some slight shifting from that sudden downpour on Sunday, perhaps a few feathers less. But it was still clean: the bones, the shiny sleekness of some feathers, the fluffy billow of others.

"That's weird. Still no clue what kind of bird it might be?" Mark scrutinized the remains, hovering just above them on his haunches.

"Maybe a falcon of some sort." June said. "Hard to tell, with it plucked like that."

"And how did it get like that?" Mark wondered.

"It's just like one of your mysteries!" Kate happily declared, watching them from the gravel road, unwilling to poke around in dead animal parts.

"Yes," June's smile was thin and tired. "Just."

■ ■ ■

For their last meal together, June grilled Silver Queen corn and local heritage pork chops from the farmer's market, along with thick spears of zucchini from her garden; she arranged slabs of the heirloom tomatoes picked two days ago and ripened on the kitchen windowsill, lightly salting them— they needed nothing else. She brought over a decanted bottle of 2000 Bourdeaux she had saved for a special occasion, and Mark and Kate set the table. As they sat and dishes were passed, June started to pour for them.

"Only a small taste for me, thanks," Kate said.

That sweet, dumb little thing. As if June hadn't noticed how Mark poured wine for himself and June as they ate dinner or watched a movie, but never Kate— how she hadn't touched the pots of coffee June and Mark worked their way through steadily in the mornings.

"How far along are you?" June asked.

"*Mom.*" Mark was mortified.

Kate beamed in surprise. "It's early, still. We didn't want to make it a big deal or anything, yet. I lost the last one."

June felt, rather than saw, their hands clutch under the table; she knew the shape and weight of their grief, the days of blood and tissue and loss that leaked out of the body. Protracted, pulled out, so much for what should have amounted to so little, pound for pound.

"Last time it didn't get far enough, so we didn't get around to asking you—"

"It's a boy." Her son interjected.

"Yes, a boy, and...are there any family names? Mark couldn't remember anyone beyond the most immediate family, but none of them sounded quite right. Mark's father suggested naming the baby after Uncle Frank, but, well—we've heard the stories about him, and after the way he behaved at the wedding..."

June softened, as if something had been splayed open inside her. "Hugh," she told them.

"Who's that?" Kate asked.

"My brother."

The girl was perplexed; Mark blank and stunned. "What brother?"

*The dogs that existed and roiled around that valley fifty years before could also announce an arrival before any noise calibrated for human ears crept fully over the ridge.*

It was the kind of deep winter cold that stabs your lungs when you take that first breath out the door. The dogs that existed and roiled around that valley fifty years before could also announce an arrival before any noise calibrated for human ears crept fully over the ridge.

But June and her parents had expected the usual when the dogs began barking that January night: the sucking open and shut of the outer mudroom door, and then a quick parting of the inner door so dogs could swarm and jump as feet were stamped free of debris, as layers were peeled off. And then her father would grumble, from his recliner, behind a book: "close the door, Hugh—you're lettin' all the warm air out."

They had expected this familiar thing, and not a knock.

"Get that, June." Her father heaved himself out of the recliner, as June quickly left her Social Studies homework on the kitchen table to open the doors. "Who's that?" Her mother called out from upstairs, folding laundry into piles on the bed.

Only the pink nose, dark mustache, and tiny red-rimmed eyes of the county sheriff peeked out from the balaklava. Sheriff Jonson was known for putting a touch of moonshine in his coffee after noon. For this, he had drunk some straight from the Mason Jar he kept tucked in the glove box.

"Miss June. Hi there, Rich."

"Eddie," her father put his hand on her shoulder, and she heard the calluses grate against her sweater.

Sheriff Jonson was still staring at June's father even as he told her, "Little lady, you best be gettin' to bed. Go on, now."

And that's what she remembered, as she turned to look from the kitchen, before heading through the living room and upstairs: Sheriff Jonson, now holding his hat in his hands in front of him, her father's hand tensing around the door knob.

Her mother's wailing started only a little later.

■ ■ ■

June did not anticipate Mark's reaction; he paced, propelled by some furnace of anger. Kate fixed her attention on the dinner dishes, desperately seeking something to do with her hands, to both be there and not for this conflagration.

June told them what she could. A night studying for an exam with a friend in town, a patch of black ice on a tight curve, and Hugh's pickup took a tumble down and over the edge of the road, flipping, and Hugh had gone through the windshield and landed just so—defying June's belief that her brother was invincible. He dispatched six-foot rattlers trying to take up residence under their front porch stairs with an axe; flung himself from a rope at the height of its arc, high above the James River; scaled rocks seemingly without holds; clambered onto the backs of surly horses and tamed them.

"It was an accident," June said, losing patience at her son's petulance. "It wasn't about genetics, there was nothing to be inherited. Nothing relevant to any medical history."

"He was my uncle," Mark spat.

"He died before I could have even conceivably had you." She didn't mean to raise her voice, but the logic was so clear, to June.

"I'm going to bed," Mark declared mid-pace. June offered up no protest, only an unreturned, "Good night."

She sat at the kitchen counter as Kate finished the last dish, softly said, "Night," and retreated upstairs.

■ ■ ■

June made her way—glass of wine in hand—to the backyard and set out the lawn chair she kept folded by the side porch. She watched as the tiny squares of light cast from the guest bath on the second floor onto the slightly overgrown grass below disappeared, and then as the lamps in Mark's old bedroom went out.

And then, she stared at the sky.

There's a certain space carved out when someone dies. Cells stop moving. Matter is not displaced: but particular motions cease, energy dissipates. A space of emptiness, of nothing, where once things took place.

She thought about these empty spaces at night: especially at night. When it was a new moon, or slow to rise, just as it was that night, she would sit on her family land with a stemless glass she could nestle in the grass beside her. The black matter between the stars, so sharp, so clear—light trickling down from centuries, eons away to shine down on her little valley.

June had a grasp of physics—knew it not to be scientifically true: but she felt that blackness echo and resonate with the lack, as if it was a buffer for the vibrant energy around it.

■ ■ ■

Elvis and Riley woke June up at five to go out—even earlier than usual: as if they sensed something in the house was amiss, and were eager to escape. She poured coffee and sat on the side porch in one of the two rocking chairs, listening the dogs' barks bounce in and around the valley, watching as the barest of glows began in the east.

The mudroom doors opened and shut, and Kate stepped out with mug of raspberry tea cupped in her hands; she slid and sat with her back rigid, unwilling to fully submit to the rocking chair.

"You should have told him," Kate finally said, after a minute of June's rocking, their eyes locked on the ridge. It was said without rancor or recrimination—just a plainly stated assertion.

"Maybe," June shrugged—surprised by her own lack of defensiveness. They watched as the pink began working its way around the edges of the mountains, like paint bleeding through thin silk paper.

"Nothing would be different, if Mark had known," June told Kate. "Nothing in his life would have changed."

Neither of them turned or changed their gaze, but from the corner of her eye June saw Kate nod twice, and then sink back into the chair. They moved slowly then, out of sync.

"Hugh's ashes are buried under that bench, up beyond the vegetables. In case you and Mark want to visit before you go."

A few minutes later, and Kate was alone on the porch, rocking.

From her bedroom window after a shower, June saw Mark and Kate holding hands up past the garden, standing in front of the bench—by the row of flame azaleas, trumpet vines wound around their branches, blazing orange and red in the fullness of the summer morning sun.

■ ■ ■

Just a bit up the slope from those azaleas, a little beyond the bench, Mark built a fort one Christmas when he was ten.

That was the last year Mark tried to feed the chickadees from his hand. Mark was a toddler when he first witnessed the voracious little things dance across his grandfather's shoulders, then hop down June's father's forearm to take sunflower seeds from his palm. Mark clapped from the porch, his three-year-old fingers splaying and never quite meeting. The chickadees refused to eat from June's father when Mark was too close; the toddler stood on the boot bench in the mudroom so as to see them swarm as the feeder was refilled, anxious breath mottling the window.

But that Christmas, a ten-year-old Mark refused his gloves, hoping to feel the light scrapes of chickadee feet. June watched his ministrations from the warmth of the house. Mark positioned himself near the feeder, barely moving for up to ten minutes some days: switching the mound of sunflower seed from one palm to the other when his fingers started to freeze, shoving the empty hand in his coat pocket—holding his breath every time one braver chickadee worked its way down to the lowest-hanging branch of the ash tree. Eventually he would grow bored and retreat to the woods, dragging dead limbs and brush down to edge of the yard, about twenty feet up from the row of azaleas.

"When can I see it?" June asked every afternoon as Mark unbundled.

"It's not *ready*, Mom."

"Patience is a virtue, June," her mother chided from behind a crossword puzzle, a book. At the week's close, Mark knocked the snow off his boots along the mudroom sill, but didn't cross the threshold into the house proper, bellowing—"Come see!" He dragged his boots through the last bits of slushy snow from the night's few inches on the porch steps, waiting for the women to pull on their winter gear. His grandfather was in town, fetching groceries and seed.

The fort was lopsided on the western end, and the eastern side was only saved from toppling due to a strong horizontal

*He dragged his boots through the last bits of slushy snow from the night's few inches on the porch steps, waiting for the women to pull on their winter gear.*

brace: a thick piece of cedar, unfinished, two-feet wide and three long, at least six inches thick. June saw the furrows of dirt and snow where the plank had been pushed and flipped up the slope, stripped from the foot-high stone and cement pillars below the azaleas.

"Mark." Something in June's tone made Mark stop mid-motion, arms sweeping towards his architectural feat. "Why'd you take that from the bench?"

June's mother halted in the last few steps to the structure, the ruddiness of winter draining from her face.

"No one ever sits there," Mark said—not a challenge, just a fact. "You can't do that."

"I was gonna put it back—"

"You *can't* do that. That bench is special to Grandma."

"Why?" A childhood of *whys*, but it was only now that June felt reason fraying, with words she couldn't give shape or form to.

"It just *is*." Guilt, confusion, suspicion, flitted across her son's face. It was as if she had drawn a demarcation of sorts there between them, like making a line in the dirty snow with a brittle piece of pine.

"It's okay, Mark," his grandmother assured him, her voice low, and heavy with the forgiving. "I never told you it was special."

Mark didn't ask again; he took the fort apart the next day, returning the remnants back into the forest, the cedar to its stone and cement supports.

■ ■ ■

On the ride back to the station, June and Mark managed to pretend the fight never happened, and Kate delicately obliged, keeping the conversation safe and quotidian. They took turns embracing at the station—and surely, they asked June, she'd be up to see the baby and their new house? "Of course."

■ ■ ■

The next morning, June took a dose of her arthritis medication before starting up the mountain. Even from the gravel road, she could see that the pile had shrunk. Up close, the feathers had crusted together with grime, the bones were muddied and dull, and a whiff of deterioration rose from the mass. Even though it was worse on her knees, she knew she'd take the logging road back after she summited, so as to avoid the pile—hoping it would somehow fold and collapse into the dirt before her next hike.

Back at the house, June reheated a cup of coffee, and then sat down to catch up on emails she largely avoided during the visit; at the top of the inbox was an attachment from Kate, sent only an hour ago.

An image: greys and blacks cut through with white contours, and only a line of text below: "Say hello to baby Hugh." ■

# ON MOTHER'S DAY

I'm going to pretend
that mine ain't dead,
that she just got Corona.

Because she was a nurse
I know she'd be very serious
about social distancing,
hand washing, and the wearing
of masks.

So me and my siblings would
probably plant ourselves
six feet apart
in her back yard,
so that when she got up to
open her blinds and stepped out
onto her balcony
into the sunshine
we'd all be sitting there
in our lawn chairs, smiling.

Somebody would lead us
in a song which we'd sing
badly, but with all our hearts.

She would blow us kisses
and rain down i love you's.

We'd linger until she made us go
or some other mother's Day
pulled us away.

Folks are going to be salty
and complain all day about not
getting to hug their mamas.

Believe me when I tell you,
I really understand.

**FRANK X WALKER**

# HAIRLINE FRACTURE

*for Taajwar*

Now that shelter-at-home
has passed the three-week mark,
I look in the mirror and smile
when I see my grandfather's hairline.
I also see my grown man son staring back
and very little of me, since I've been mostly bald
for over thirty years—longer than he's been alive.

But not a primping and preening son
who would ever worry about anything as superficial
as hair, but a Vulcan-like logic son who in response
to uninvited compliments on his new-look beard
in the much coveted Tokyo pictures the twins found
on social media, quickly said, in his defense,

"I joined an on-line group called 'Black in Japan'
and asked, but there are no products in the stores
and no black barbers anywhere near me."

It made me laugh then and running my fingers across
my dome reminds me even now, that I may
or may not partake in some groom for Zoom
today, before throwing on a hat, to distinguish myself
from him and my father's father, however slightly.

I have not seen the inevitable plethora of Corona
t-shirts yet, but I'll be looking for one that says,
This hairy beast is not the pandemic me
—I'm just missing my son.

**FRANK X WALKER**

# DEEJAY BATTLE

*"When the looting starts, the shooting starts."*
                                    *—president DJ Trump*

The oppressors' private property
is always more important
to the privileged. That power
is what police protect.

Backed by a national guard
fronting a commander-in-cheat
known to incite and encourage
violence against POC by the FOP
and other 'good people' vs 'THUGS'

If you don't understand
this behavior
or these people
you don't understand
emotional or psychological trauma.
You don't understand
generational grief.

And you really don't understand
injustice or American history.

Know justice. Know peace.
No justice. No peace.
No just ICE raids.
No guilty cops, just us,
dead, dying, and chalk marked
over and over again,

like some wack DJ, rewinding
the bridge or dead refrain,
scratching at our eyes

with already viral
breathless black body porn
professionally made
by the hands, feet and now knees
of thug police again

instead of turning the tables
we drag out turntables
and spin and spin and spin
searching old wax, seeking to sample
something human,
anything truly good to mix
with this black,
with this life,
until we matter.

**FRANK X WALKER**

# Y'ALL SAY I DO, WE SAY BLACK LIVES MATTER

*for Kerry and Michael*

What a powerful way to say 'til death
do us part. To stand in defiance of murder
after murder after murder and still choose life,
together. To seal your vows and then march

for all our promises, into Philly streets,
swollen with protestors, they replaced thrown rice
with tear gas and pepper spray, but it still felt
more like a large reception for freedom than a riot.

Resplendent in wedding gown and tuxedo,
fists raised high to demonstrate that
Black Love is the Liberation married
to the joy that fills your faces,

thinking only of the honeymoon where all couples
know justice because Black couples know peace.

**FRANK X WALKER**

# MRS. BUTTERWORTH, UNCLE BEN, & AUNT JEMIMA

...walk into a bar in America.
Butterworth says, I'm being repackaged.
Ben says, I'm being rebranded.
And Jemima says, I remember
when they branded my mama     on her back.
The bartender says, I could stand in the middle
of Main Street and kill somebody
and I wouldn't lose any voters.
Butterworth says, then I'll take eight bullets
in my sleep. Ben says choke me to death
with your knee. And Jemima says,
lock me in a holding cell and say
I decided to hang myself.
The bartender poured the drinks,
said he felt threatened,
and was simply standing his ground.
He said he thought the thug
was reaching for a gun.
The headlines said Well-Loved American
Foods Resisted Arrest, Failed
to Comply, and Were Delicious While Black.
Butterworth's daughter said here's to progress
we might finally get an anti-lynching bill.
Ben's son said I'd rather they abolish
qualified immunity. Jemima's kid said you know
they abolished slavery once,
then they hung my mama     on that box.

**FRANK X WALKER**

# BAPTISM BY DIRT

*for Shauna*

All believers know about the power of water
though not enough recognize the power of dirt.
My mama used to walk barefooted
in our vegetable garden,
get down on her hands and knees
and almost pray in the dirt.
My wife and I and our two-year old
built and planted three raised-bed gardens.
Watching her dip her fingers into the dirt
to coddle what will feed us
reminds me of mama and then.
What is it that women know
about nurturing a seed into a piece of fruit,
about believing in the power of dirt
and suns and water?
I return from our labor with sore knees
and back, fingernails and hands caked with dirt.
She floats back into the house somehow cleaner
almost burdenless,
as if she spent the weekend
burying all her heavy things,
as if she whispered to something sacred
and it whispered something back.

**FRANK X WALKER**

# COMMENCEMENT 2020

*"...ground yourself in values that last, like honesty,*
*hard work, responsibility, fairness, generosity,*
*[and] respect for others."*

*—President Barack Obama*

I have a grandson in the class of 2020,
the first high school class born after 9/11.
Yo-Yo Ma played "Simple Gifts"
and a little Bach No. 6 on national TV for him
and all his classmates across the country.

And as if just to prove my age, Ma was followed
by a slate of musicians I had never heard of
with names like Dua Lipa, Bad Bunny, and H.E.R.

A whole platoon of famous athletes, actors,
musicians, CEO's and former presidents
showed up to congratulate them,
to applaud their advocacy and service, to salute
their passion, resilience, patience and creativity,
to send them off, to urge them to "demand better,"
to officially hand them the keys to the future.

And why not? Who else has inherited so many
school shootings? Who else has been more invested
in climate change? Who else uses our terrifying work
tools as toys to consume TikTok?

After three years of the current administration,
its anti-education Secretary of Education,

and Zoom physics and calculus, they need no mandate
to change the world.

They already started with at-home proms,
drive-in theater graduations and middle of main
street parade-style processionals. Only parents
are afraid they'll spend the best years of college
the same way they finished senior year.

In truth, adults have broken a lot of shit.
Let's not get in the way while they endeavor to fix it.

This class will be forever special if for no other reason,
despite the partisan divide modeled by adults,
the whole damn country graduated together.

**FRANK X WALKER**

# SECONDHAND STORIES

REBECCA HAZELWOOD

**M**ost summer Saturday nights of my childhood, I snuggled in the crook of Granny Gracie's bare legs, just the two of us watching *The Golden Girls* on the big box TV in her living room, taking lessons from Blanche Devereaux. When Blanche mentioned being as jumpy as a virgin at a prison rodeo, I said, "Granny, what's a virgin?" She said, "Well, you know honey, that's when a woman hasn't slept with a man."

Granny was an expert in courting, only forty-six when I was born and still hot to trot. She wore satin nightgowns on humid summer nights and red, fuzzy onesie pajamas on nights after the frost arrived in Kentucky. The rest of her was always the same, no matter the season: red toenails and pink fingernails, with a hunk of Super Glue under at least one nail that she'd broken while doing the housework. My northerner mother was first shocked and then amused when she learned Granny's secret for keeping her long nails; she used to hold up Granny's hands and peer underneath her nails every time we visited, just to check for the Super Glue. Granny never disappointed. Every Friday morning, she got her short hair curled and hairsprayed at the beauty shop in Berea, and the rest of the week she slept on a satin pillowcase to keep her hair in shape. She never washed it herself if she could help it. In the morning, she'd pick out the flattened hair in the back and hairspray it again. I must've watched her do this hundreds of times. My father always said Granny's hair looked like a bird's nest, but she never had any trouble finding a man. Granny was kind of glamorous.

Though we lived an hour away in Frankfort, the Kentucky state capital where my father was a cop, my parents took me to Granny's house nearly every weekend of my childhood. I spent many hours in the backseat of our car with a coloring book or a chapter book as my father took Versailles Road out to the interstate, east on I-64 and south along I-75, passing hills and horse farms and barns, over the Kentucky River to the Clays Ferry truck stop, the halfway point where Granny waited for us in her Toyota station wagon we called the "yellow banana." The world was so large then, a mystery, full of big bridges and tall semis and young Granny in her slim jeans and spaghetti-strap tops.

As I've gotten older, I've started to think about Granny more, letting her story sharpen and come into focus as if through a camera lens. When Granny was a young woman, she lived down by the railroad tracks in a leaning two-story white house on Maple Street, with low ceilings and uneven, red-carpeted floors. Granny says she got the carpet in a bargain bin; the whole house consisted of things nobody else wanted. She had four kids with a husband who ran away to Florida with another woman and then drank himself to death at forty—a decade before I was born. Granny never had anything nice to say about him, so she often said nothing at all. But her kids say he only came home long enough to knock her up or knock her around for being mouthy. On her own, Granny had no car and she worked in a factory making gauges—but she never called it a factory. She always talked about working at Dresser or "down at the plant," so I never imagined her on an assembly line. When she got paid on Friday, the four kids got a six-pack of pop as a treat. By Wednesday of the next week, the money always ran out and the kids were left to scavenge for food with relatives and neighbors until Friday came round again.

Granny was still living on Maple Street when I was born, but I barely remember the house. It survives in secondhand stories. As the oldest child, my father was expected to make his brothers and sister mind. If the house wasn't clean when Granny got home from work, she blamed him, screaming and throwing salt and pepper shakers at his head. Sometimes she left for work on Friday morning and didn't come home until Monday after work, partying with her friends. The kids didn't know if she was dead or alive for days at a time. Sometimes I have trouble reconciling my father's stories with the Granny I know, but I have never asked her about it. She has always been reluctant to talk about the past, especially when it is ugly.

■ ■ ■

Just after I turned thirty-two, Granny Gracie and I met for
a birthday lunch. We hadn't talked in nearly a year—despite
the fact that I lived just an hour down the road. We'd had a
big fight because I was unemployed and miserable, but when
I called Granny to make up, she said we didn't have to talk
about it. We could just move on. We decided to meet at our
place, PapaLeno's, an old Italian family restaurant in the Berea
town square with big wide windows and soft open light—and
butter-soaked garlic bread as big as my forearm. After we sat
down, I decided to tell Granny and her boyfriend Rex that I'd
finally made plans after nearly two years of unemployment. I'd
applied to six PhD programs in English. They were all out of
state, all four- or five-year programs. Three had waitlisted me,
two rejected me, and one accepted me. Granny nodded, cutting
into the stromboli sandwich she was sharing with Rex. "Just
think," she said, "you'll be forty without ever having a job."

I tried not to cry and instead I reminded her that I'd had
jobs before, teaching English in a French middle school,
working for a nonprofit, and teaching college English classes
while in graduate school. But none of that seemed enough.
She reminded me that she'd worked for fifty cents an hour to
support four kids. She'd worked forty hours a week for forty
years. She kept talking while I tried not to cry, telling me
about the successes of other family members, their houses
and cars and jobs and spouses and children. I didn't have any
of that, except an eleven-year-old car with peeling paint and
a loud grinding sound in the wheel well. She told me about
how much my aunt Lori and her husband cleared every month
after they paid their bills. But she didn't ask me anything else
about my plans. When I started crying too hard to chew my
ravioli, she said, "Aren't you so glad we're back together? I am."

I nodded, continuing to cry. She might never be proud of me.

■ ■ ■

In southeastern Kentucky there is an old country road miles from the nearest city. Alongside runs fading black fences to keep the livestock in and the visitors out. The road dips and sways and turns hard on a dime, like a rollercoaster. The road leads to Great-Granny Rose's two-story, eight-room farmhouse, with white siding and a septic tank outside and a great big gas heater inside. There is no air conditioning. The floors are uneven and the ceilings are low; the upstairs bedroom isn't insulated and its ceiling is made of cardboard. Out back is an old barn, some chicken coops, and a pond. Hills and hills.

*Everyone says Andy was good to Granny, taking her to Hawaii and buying her gold jewelry. Everyone loved him—everyone but me.*

This is where Granny Gracie grew up. Where the tobacco was planted and the livestock was raised. Pigs, cows, chickens. This is what Granny Gracie dropped out of school for in the eighth or ninth grade: Bear Wallow, an unincorporated community on the western edge of Appalachia in Madison County, Kentucky.

I often think about Bear Wallow, especially when I am trying to understand Granny Gracie. I don't know what led her to the leaning white house on Maple Street in Berea with four kids. But when I was six, she married her neighbor Andy, a World War II veteran with a missing arm, and they moved into a three-bedroom brick house in a subdivision on the edge of Berea. The floors were even and the house didn't lean. They even had a carport. Everyone says Andy was good to Granny, taking her to Hawaii and buying her gold jewelry. Everyone loved him—everyone but me.

I remember the day he stood up from the kitchen table in the new brick house and yelled in front of me, telling Granny what a brat I was. I was only six or seven or eight, a little bratty but not deserving of his anger. I hated him after that, but I never wondered if this was indicative of how he treated Granny, too. Now we never talk about him, unless we are looking through old photo albums; even a Polaroid of Granny in a bikini and Andy in Speedos taken in Fort Lauderdale in 1987 doesn't prompt much commentary, though they actually look happy. After Andy died less than two years into their marriage, Granny kept his last name and the house, where we watched TV on Saturday nights.

Granny is in her eighties now, and she's settled in the house she bought with Andy. It has two window air conditioners—one in the kitchen and one in Granny's back bedroom—and beige carpeting, a washer and dryer in the bathroom, and a tiny koi pond out back. Granny's got cranberry Fenton glass on display and curio cabinets full of decorative teapots and a fancy ornamental chamber pot in the living room. She's got at least one Paul Sawyer print—probably a gift from my father, who collected the limited-edition prints from the Kentucky painter—and a gold-framed mirror on the living room wall. She's stuffed all three bedroom closets full of clothes of every color, mostly for church, and cluttered every bedroom doorknob with several hangers full of clothes—on both sides of the door. Her wooden armoire is so full that it doesn't close on its own; she has a thick rubber band keeping the knobs together and the doors closed. But the beds are always made and the house is always white-glove clean.

Sometimes, when we're together and I don't know what to talk about with Granny, I study her gold jewelry. Granny Gracie's got ropes of gold dangling from her neck, so many necklaces stacked on top of each other that she can't take them off at night, and most have solid gold pendants: a nugget, a flip flop, a plumeria flower, a hula dancer from Hawaii with moving legs. A tangle of gold bracelets hangs from her wrists, most of them from boyfriends after Andy died: Joe, Monroe, Rex. Granny used to have a gold ring on every finger, multiple rings of diamond clusters, until the skin cancers and blood thinners made her hands too sensitive. Some of them she bought on layaway at Walmart or Kmart, some came from boyfriends. At last count, she was only wearing eleven gold rings on her fingers.

When I was a child, Granny used to give me my own gold. She taught me to love solid gold, to snub my nose at gold-plated jewelry because it wore so easily, and to judge by the karats. I never knew what karats indicated, but I parroted the language. Now I know that twenty-four-karat is the purest, but it's too soft and malleable for most jewelry, too easily bent or scratched. It's usually only traded and stockpiled for wealth. Most gold jewelry is eighteen or fourteen or ten-karats, gold mixed with other metals to harden it. I lost every ten-karat gold ring Granny bought me, most of them in gas station bathrooms, always forgetting to put the rings on again after washing my hands. Sometimes I chipped the prongs holding the stones in my rings, losing pink ice or sapphire stones. I was a clumsy child. I wonder how many layaway payments she had to make for each ring I lost.

My maternal grandmother complains that Granny's jewelry is gaudy, so excessive and flashy, but I know Granny is only making up for the years she couldn't afford food, let alone jewelry. I have similar impulses to make up for the past, but I buy designer handbags with my student loan money instead. Granny still tries to give me gold jewelry that she doesn't want—a pair of gold hoop earrings, a gold and ruby pinky ring—and shoes she picks up in yard sales. But I don't wear gold jewelry and she often buys the wrong size of shoes; nevertheless, she looks hurt when I don't take what she offers. I wish she'd save her money. The only thing I want—the solid gold hula dancer pendant—will go to my aunt Lori, Granny Gracie says.

■ ■ ■

Granny never talks about how well she's done for herself or her decision to move from Bear Wallow, though most of her brothers and sisters stayed there, only moving to neighboring towns and states for short periods of their lives but almost always returning to the trailers and houses built on Great-Granny Rose's land—or just up the road. Only her sister Mafre built a life and a family in Cincinnati. Granny Gracie never talks about dropping out of school, either. When I was a child, it only slipped out once.

I remember the Sunday afternoon sitting under Granny Gracie's carport in Berea after Andy died, the sun a watercolor stain on the sky, my mother and father lighting up cigarette after cigarette and drinking instant coffee. A smoke cloud hovered under the awning. My father's Air Force buddy and his family were visiting, and someone mentioned that Granny had dropped out of school in the eighth or ninth grade. She nodded, confirming it, but she didn't say anything else. No one had ever mentioned it before, or maybe I'd never paid attention. I was probably only eight-years-old. Later that evening, my father's Air Force buddy asked me what I thought of my granny. "She's craaaaazy," I said, echoing what my father said at home, away from Granny Gracie. I thought I was being funny, performing as expected. Everyone but Granny laughed, and I could tell that I hurt her feelings, which I hadn't anticipated. When my parents took me home that night, my mother prompted me to call Granny Gracie from the rotary phone in our kitchen and apologize.

"I'm not going to forgive you," Granny said. But she never mentioned it again.

■ ■ ■

Granny Gracie says she wishes we were close like we used to be, and I can remember taking a trip with her down to South Carolina to see my aunt Lori when I was still a child. Granny drove us down I-75 and across I-40 in her yellow banana station wagon, just the two of us crossing the Smokies. Somewhere in the mountains, Granny let me eat something sticky, some caramel or taffy, and my baby molar nearly fell out, only hanging on like a hinge.

"Lord god, keep that thing in there," Granny commanded from the driver's seat. "Your parents will kill me for letting you eat that." I pushed the tooth up with my tongue the whole way there and back, waiting to see a dentist until I got home. I didn't want to get Granny in trouble.

Later, after I went off to college, I rarely stayed with Granny, but we were still close except when she'd fuss at me for drinking. On Christmas, my aunt Lori would give me male butt calendars, and Granny and I would flip through the months. Granny would raise her eyebrows and twirl her eyes at each new set of buns, calling out "Woo, woo!" We were both boy crazy, though Granny was always the one with a boyfriend. When we stayed at my aunt Lori's house, we often played Phase 10 until Granny cheated, swapping out her useless cards with ones she needed when no one was looking. She'd get a big grin on her face like a gurgling baby, giving herself away, and she'd inevitably confess.

Sometimes when I am missing Granny, I ride the roads of Madison County, using Internet maps from four states away, where I am getting my PhD in English. I start in Bear Wallow, on the road my family lived on for generations, five miles from the nearest highway. Dreyfus Road leads to Battlefield Memorial Highway and then onto 1016, a ten-mile path to the edge of Berea from Bear Wallow. The two-lane roads are penned in by fences and telephone poles and electricity lines, trees and houses, old trailers and tiny dirty shacks with basketball hoops and huge new brick houses with multiple-car

*I trace the roads when I am homesick for the hills and mountains, the bumps and turns on the roads that cut through them. I am trying to figure out how we got here.*

garages set far back from the road. There are stark white holiness churches and country store markets with one gas pump and auction houses with homemade signs along the road, bursts of life to break up the backcountry nothingness. This is the road to Granny Gracie's house in Berea, the path she must've traveled as a young woman when she left home. I trace the roads when I am homesick for the hills and mountains, the bumps and turns on the roads that cut through them. I am trying to figure out how we got here.

I think it started six Christmases ago, when I was twenty-nine. I walked into Granny Gracie's living room and my aunt Lori pointed her new 9mm Smith and Wesson—a Christmas present from her husband—at me. No one said anything. Maybe they were so busy unwrapping presents or playing with toys that they didn't notice, or maybe they didn't care. There was no one reason for my aunt Lori to point her gun at me, just a growing tension on that side of the family. Nevertheless, Lori's behavior went unnoticed; it was only on the drive home that my mother confirmed I hadn't imagined the gun pointed at me. Then, a month and a half later, my father was arrested for growing marijuana in his trailer; he'd moved back to Bear Wallow after my parents divorced.

I think it started when I panicked, realizing the crash and confluence of events showed who we were and always would be: dark, violent, unhappy. I didn't want to be a part of that anymore. I cut ties with my aunt Lori first, then my father, and moved from Georgia—where I was finishing an MFA in creative writing—to Kentucky, to Chicago, and then back again to Kentucky, trying to escape something that felt like destiny. I was mostly unemployed for over two years, always in a constant state of panic about what I was doing with my life, like a hummingbird burning through fuel while searching for food. It started when I failed to imagine how this would affect my relationship with Granny.

Families are as vast and complex and interconnected as the human body—even dysfunctional families. We share blood, after all. If one part stops working, the rest of the body suffers, like a malfunctioning pancreas that stops producing insulin and causes diabetes. The extra sugar spreads out through the bloodstream, affecting every organ, every limb. You can go blind. You can lose a foot. If you are stubborn and fail to take care of the problem, you can lose your life.

When I stopped talking to my aunt and my father, I suffered from a failure of imagination about the ways we were connected. It wasn't just that some of my family members quietly chose sides, fading from my life. It wasn't just that I spent Thanksgiving and Christmas apart from Granny, since I was the one who stopped circulating our blood. Some of my family members haunted my online presence, too, reporting back to Granny my activities and words, commenting, "Look what your granddaughter says"—and it didn't matter if what I said was malicious or innocuous. Blocking them from my accounts and changing usernames didn't deter them. After months of this, Granny called me to say, "You're telling lies on me." Both of us cried on the phone until I got mad, explaining that she was getting secondhand information, twisted and manipulated to upset her.

"You don't have to listen to what they say. Just change the subject," I said.

"I try to, but they just keep talking," Granny said.

For nearly a year, until just after my thirty-second birthday, I stopped answering the phone when she called.

■ ■ ■

Since the beginning, Granny Gracie has tried to be a peacekeeper, neutral ground for all of us. On my thirty-second birthday lunch at PapaLeno's, she stressed how much my aunt Lori loved me. For the sake of honesty, I showed her an essay I'd written about the 9mm Smith and Wesson, and Granny said, "I'm not going to comment on that because I wasn't there."

She'd been in the next room.

"I don't know why anybody would want to read this," she said. "It's not interesting. I wasn't interested in reading that."

I was hurt by her criticism of my writing, but I knew it was hard for her to read such ugliness. I knew she didn't want me to publish it, make it public. Then she said softly, "I'm sorry you had to live through that."

Granny said she'd forgiven my father for everything he's done, for a lifetime of vices and rage, affairs and drugs and booze. "He couldn't help it," she said. "He was on drugs." But when I tried to explain what he was like as a father, how much of a hold he'd had on me, the harsh and critical words he'd used, she simply said, "He's your daddy."

"He's not my daddy," I said.

"He's your daddy."

"He's not my daddy," I said. "He's my father."

"Well, fine, but he's your father."

I knew I was being nitpicky about language. I knew family meant everything to her, and that was why she loved me despite everything. But I also knew we were repeating the same violence and unhappiness, generation after generation, and I wanted to break the pattern. I wanted something new.

■ ■ ■

Sometimes when I visit Granny, she lets me drive her down Scaffold Cane Road, past the small older houses and trailers, empty fields, and Baptist churches, to Fentress Lane, where her in-laws lived. My great Grandpa Hazelwood built onto the one-room house, room by room, adding upstairs bedrooms and a railed-in porch. After my last great uncle died, the house passed out of our hands, and the new owners have curious taste. Granny wrinkles her nose as we pass the red tin roof and all the campers in the yard. At the house down the road, she swears they trade drugs for cars; they have at least twenty old cars in the yard. And then we turn around.

Inevitably, we head for Granny's old white house. The house on Maple Street has been demolished now, the lean-to worth less than the land it was on, down among the railroad tracks and warehouse buildings. All that remains of the original is a concrete square where the kitchen used to be. Before a duplex was built on the site, Granny Gracie and I would drive by the vacant lot and she'd point out the small square of kitchen floor, but it was always so much smaller than I remembered. Still, we drive by even now, looking for who we are. ■

# BEERSHEBA SPRINGS ASSEMBLY

*Grundy County, Tennessee*

I agreed to go in the fall, discouraged
by my own frailty and humanness,
my marriage a hollow, soured thing,
cracked covenant frayed at the root.
I was thirsty. Bereft. It's why I came
to this place where a woman named
Beersheba once discovered a chalybeate
spring and who else should have found
it but her? a woman named for the spot
where Abraham dug a well in the desert
then honored the oath he and Abimelech
made, a place of shade and exile, freshly
planted tamarisks and seven sent away
lambs, perhaps not altogether unlike
these grounds built and tended by
hands never free to do as they chose—
the quiet, linen furnished rooms
where we sleep and meditate and
pray purchased with sin's wages,
hundreds adding up to thousands
of bodies crammed together in ships,
legs bound with iron chains, blistered
feet marched mile after mile, winding
through the Shenandoah deeper south,
women, men, and children chained
and raped and beat and through all
that unending horror forced to sing,
cloying songs of hope sticking to
the sides of their swollen tongues

and mosquito bit parched mouths.
Tonight, as we're asked to stand
and finish the evening service with
one last hymn, I find myself
looking out past the frail, sturdy
arms of the cross to the lashed
open back of the valley below,
the mountains all around us
trembling wound, bathed in
the cold narrow light of
God's turned away face.

**JENN BLAIR**

# AFTER THE PRODIGAL RETURNED

he kept at his big-chest
strutting around, waving
his bestiality in our faces,
chuckling at those of us
whose hands had stuck to
the plow, stupid, plodding
animals with no imagination
but to obey. Even in the
pews his eyes shone with
rank pride as he gazed out
the glass, peering beyond
lichen draped gravestones
to something half-coiled
and wanton basking in the
butter slathered sun. A
few weeks later, his parents
invited us all to the fatted-
calf feast—a hog yanked
out of the woods, its throat
promptly slit on behalf of
one who almost missed the
meal prayer on account of
his having gone behind
the smokehouse to regale
some young impressionables
with tales of his most recent
exploits. Handed my meagre
portion I meekly nodded
my thanks then went over
to a nearby stump and sat

there by myself quietly
chewing, ruing all the golden
autumn afternoons the
charred flesh on my plate
might have spent snuffling
yet for chestnut and acorn
scattered across the forest floor,
its dripping snout quivering,
full of honest enjoyment.

**JENN BLAIR**

# HELLBENDER

she shucked her eyes.
left her tongue. took it off,
set it on a flat granite rock
for ravens to peck/salamanders
to roost as she walked further
and further into the woods,
hands cupped to catch
whatever small speckles
of light could manage to
filter all the way down
through the branches,
sifted minnows darting
across her thirsty palms.

**JENN BLAIR**

# THE FLOOD

In the small cemetery off Cherokee Road
two women in sweat-stained tank tops
tame what's grown wild with a push
mower and silver clippers, busily clearing
amaranth and curled dock and yanking out
unsightly pigweed. After carefully tending
their relatives' graves, they quickly spruce
up the immediate neighbors, but then the
wild thistle swiftly resumes, no intended slight.

It's just that they have family waiting back
at home, children impatient to salvage
whatever's left of this hot, humid Saturday,
the work they leave here another reminder
that even the widest act of mercy must leave
anguish at its edges, Noah and his kin safely
embracing inside the clearing while everyone else's
stone slowly disappears beneath the lengthening grass.

**JENN BLAIR**

# PAPERS

Byron Herbert Reece (1917-1958)

Whatever was going to happen next must have
been temporarily pushed aside to concentrate
on the missing comma/comma splice/awkward
run-on sentence spilling over line after line/the
painfully overeager student's usual too much fullness
/any attempted meaning jumbled in an ocean of
intensifiers while the perpetually distracted boy
who sat in the back row adjusting his tan watch
band for the better part of the hour would do
well to elucidate: "Interesting. See if you can develop
this point a little further." One of the three papers
he stapled together belonged to the perfectionist
who, almost in tears, had profusely apologized.
Adding an introductory colon to a dropped quote,
he reminded himself again not to skew too low
or high, overindulge in wrath or forgiveness,
even if the number alone decided if its eventual
recipient felt more sorrow or scorn when the news
broke. The brilliant girl who wore ill-fitting blouses
the color of egg yoke and a perpetual scowl:
*And why should the dead judge me?* He usually didn't
bother to correct it—the familiar misspelling
of his name, but this time, decided to strike a line
through the unnecessary "s," the new blue "c"
floating above it one last small nod to himself.
He barely noticed them anymore—coffee-rings,
apple-flecks, salt-smears, water droplets harvested
from an exuberant sneeze. But for all they gave
him he had not asked, it wouldn't be fair to mar

their thoughts, awkwardly phrased or no, with
merciless red marks. After stacking the papers
up in a neat pile, he placed them in his top desk
drawer, shutting it all the way, to keep them safe,
then stood, crossing the room to the small shelf
holding the campus apartment's record player,
scratched needle already positioned right before
the note Mozart rips open the slumbering air.

**JENN BLAIR**

AN *APPALACHIAN REVIEW*
INTERVIEW

# CARTER SICKELS

In January, as he walked through the crowded streets of Park City, Utah, Carter Sickels's year looked set. The film adaptation of his debut novel *The Evening Hour* had just premiered to critical buzz at the Sundance Film Festival. Praise was already rolling in for his second novel *The Prettiest Star*, which was slated to be published in May. Set in 1986, the book tells the story of Brian Jackson, a gay man from rural Ohio who seeks freedom and acceptance in New York City. But after losing his lover to AIDS and facing the prospect of his own death, he returns to the family and place he left behind to confront his past and future.

Earlier this spring, as the country moved into lockdown due to the COVID-19 pandemic, Sickels discussed the book in a series of emails with fellow novelist Robert Gipe. In the conversation that follows, edited for length and clarity, Sickels reflects on his inspirations for the novel, the AIDS crisis in rural America, how he conjured the 1980s on the page, when we can expect to see the film of *The Evening Hour*, and the parallels he sees between our present moment and the world of *The Prettiest Star*.

■ ■ ■

**ROBERT GIPE: Why did you write *The Prettiest Star*?**

**CARTER SICKELS:** It was an idea I'd written down, just one idea of many, for a short story or a novel: an HIV-positive man returns to his hometown in the mid-eighties during the AIDS epidemic. I didn't know if the idea had legs or not, but I kept coming back to it. I started thinking about Jess, Brian's little sister, and how it would feel to have her brother come back. Brian's voice started to speak to me too. Then, I thought about the family and the town, and the stigma surrounding queerness and AIDS. I also remembered watching this episode of [*The Oprah Winfrey Show*], when I was a teenager, about a gay man who was HIV-positive, and went swimming in his hometown public swimming pool in West Virginia; when he got in the pool, everyone else got out, the mayor drained the pool, and he was barred from coming back. That stuck with me, too. It happened in 1987.

**Carter Sickels**

I wanted to tell a story about the AIDS crisis—this time of America that so many young people don't know much about, this critical moment in queer and American history—and look at it through the lens of rural America.

**RG: Tell us about the research behind *The Prettiest Star*. How did you prepare to write about that time and place?**

CS: I conducted a lot of research about the AIDS crisis in the eighties. I read everything from seminal texts like *And the Band Played On* by Randy Shilts to magazines articles in *Life* and *People*. I looked at art from that period, like the work of David Wojnarowicz, and the photographs of Nan Goldin, and watched documentaries and videos.

One particular influence on my novel was [the memoir] *My Own Country* by Abraham Varghese, about Varghese's years as an infectious disease doctor in east Tennessee, where he treated some of the area's first AIDS patients. It's the only book, at least that I'm aware of, that examines the AIDS crisis of the eighties and nineties in rural America. Varghese portrays the deep isolation people felt, people who often didn't have familial or community support, or resources, with tenderness and complexity.

I also drew on my own memories and immersed myself in eighties pop culture by listening to a lot of music and watching music videos, TV shows, commercials. The Internet makes that kind of research super easy, but physical objects also hold major memory power. I ordered Sears and JCPenney's catalogues from eBay, and searched antique and secondhand stores for old copies of *TV Guide*, and those were excellent resources for transporting me back to that time.

**RG: What, if anything, surprised you in your research?**

**CS:** I knew about the cruelty and paranoia toward people with AIDS—parents requiring their sons eat dinner at a separate table, nurses or aides leaving trays of food in the hospital hallways, or parents not claiming their son's body from the morgue. But, I have to say, I was disturbed to read about funeral homes refusing to bury the bodies. I even read about one place that sealed the body in glass. Were they afraid the other corpses would be infected? That kind of fear grows out of a deep hatred that seemed to be about keeping queer bodies out of every public space, including cemeteries.

Honestly, in all the research, I was more surprised by the small acts of kindness and support toward people with AIDS that I came across. Parents taking in their gay son, or a woman, who, despite her preacher's hellfire and brimstone sermons, delivered food to a queer couple in town.

**RG: What part of the world of this book was the hardest for you to create? What part came easiest?**

**CS:** I grew up in the eighties, so I felt comfortable writing about the time period. The sense of place—in southeastern Ohio—also came pretty easy. What was more difficult was not so much the world, but the novel's structure. Brian's video diaries, for example, took some time to figure out how to construct, how to turn something that is so visual into prose. The alternating points of view also presented challenges— deciding when to switch perspectives, or which character would narrate a particular scene.

**RG: Are there any analogies or comparisons you'd like to draw between the AIDS pandemic of the eighties and**

the COVID-19 pandemic? It's interesting to compare the reactions to the two pandemics by some of those on the religious right.

CS: This is such a tricky question because right now we're right in the midst of this global pandemic, and things are changing so rapidly from day to day. It's important to note that regarding the AIDS pandemic, we were six years into the pandemic and over 40,000 deaths before Reagan ever mentioned the word AIDS to the public. Gay people were viewed as expendable—there were many in the country happy to see that queer people were dying.

I do think, currently, we're witnessing an incompetent, cruel administration that values the stock market over human lives, and has waged a war on science. It's also interesting to look at the hold the religious right now has on this country and political leaders, a movement that found its footing in the eighties. Jerry Falwell famously said that AIDS was God's punishment for the gays, and he played a major role in garnering Christian support for Reagan. Now we have his son, a great friend of Trump's, leading college students into a mess of COVID-19 infections. I'm sure at some point, if they haven't already, the religious right will blame COVID-19 on the gays.

RG: Andrew, the gay man who stayed in southern Ohio, says "This is our work now" to Brian's mother Sharon when Brian comes home to southern Ohio to die. That exchange was very meaningful to me—the way it spoke to the way people have to make their own family, their own community when their birth families and communities reject them. I also love it because it speaks to maybe Andrew's sense of "missing out" because he wasn't living in a larger gay community—and how ready he is to assume his place as a caregiver in that larger community. And I love it because of the way it helps Sharon find her love for her son. The world they create around Brian is so beautiful. Anything you'd like to say about how and why you created that space?

CS: Thank you for bringing this up. This was important to me to write, and I hope it resonates with readers. Even if they're own families support them, I think queer people understand, collectively, what it means to be rejected by their own biological families. There are the families we're born into, and then there are families we choose and create. The queer community has been doing this for years and years— redefining families and homes, taking care of each other because our own families or societies won't. In the eighties and nineties, queers stepped in to take care of their friends and lovers, in ways that most biological families were not doing. In *The Prettiest Star*, I wanted to show how Brian's family includes his queer friends and a few members of his biological family. This newly-formed family explores one of the novel's primary questions: how do we take care of each other? Will we extend our compassion, treat each other with dignity and respect and love?

I'm glad you brought up Andrew, who was one of my favorite characters to write. Many queer people leave their hometowns for urban spaces—for community, acceptance, freedom. But there are also stories of queer people living in rural spaces and those stories don't often get told. Andrew is a gay man who never left the area, and works at Sears. He doesn't try to hide his femininity, and Andrew's mother Janey is very supportive and loving of her son. I wanted to complicate ideas about [queerness in] urban and rural spaces, and about the people who live there.

Andrew creates a shift in the Jackson family dynamics, and destabilizes the story Brian's parents want to tell about this family. Over time, Sharon, Brian's mother, who at first couldn't see Andrew beyond her own prejudices, begins to rely on him and trust him.

**RG: There are so many other strong well-drawn characters. We'd welcome any thoughts you'd have to share on the creation of Lettie, Brian, Jess, Sharon, and Travis.**

**CS:** Lettie is Brian's grandmother. When I started writing Lettie, she drew me in right away—with her dyed black hair and gaudy jewelry. As I wrote scenes from Brian's childhood, when he went door-to-door with Lettie selling Avon, or twirled around the house singing Dolly Parton, Lettie quickly emerged as the character who would love her grandson unconditionally. As the matriarch, Lettie carries a kind of power within the family, and even within the community, and so her support is significant. I wanted to include a family member for Brian who protects and accepts him. I enjoyed writing Lettie, who brings a little levity and humor to the family unit.

Brian is the main character, and this is his story—but it's also the story of his family and community. In early drafts, Brian was all rage. But, the longer I stuck with him and developed the novel, he grew more complicated and layered. The video diaries gave me a way to let him speak directly to the reader, and to frame his story in these short sections where he's at his most vulnerable and honest, but also in control of his own story. Over time, as Brian becomes sicker, these videos start to disappear—and I wanted the reader to miss his voice, to feel that loss, that grief.

Jess is fourteen, and hasn't seen her brother since she was eight. No one will tell her why he left or why he's come back. She has to navigate this adult world of secrets and shame and silence. But she's savvy and sharp, and figures out what's going on. When I'm creating characters, I try to figure out what obsesses them, their likes and dislikes, their desires, fears, or sorrows.

With Jess, I thought about what TV shows Jess, a fourteen-year-old girl in 1986, would be watching. MTV, of course, and a lot of sitcoms. But when she was younger, what shaped her? Before my family had cable or a satellite dish, we had four channels to choose from. Like most kids from that time, I watched a lot of PBS. In addition to *Sesame Street*, *Mister Rogers*, and *The Electric Company*, nature shows always seemed to be on TV. *Nova*, *Wild America*. While I was thinking about Jess's TV-watching habits, I also watched the 2013 documentary *Blackfish*, an indictment of SeaWorld's practice of raising orcas in captivity, and remembered when I was a kid, taking a trip to SeaWorld Ohio (yes, this was a real place; it closed in 2000).

What if Jess watched a lot of nature shows? What if she fell in love with killer whales, the way some girls do with horses? She's never been to the ocean, and the images on the screen, and all the books she reads about whales, transport her from small-town Ohio to the wildness and mystery of the sea. As I did more research, I started to hear Jess's voice—and her brainy knowledge of whale facts and details worked their way into the novel.

Sharon, Brian's mother, presents herself as a woman who's very put-together, who doesn't get easily rattled. She keeps her house in order—she's always cleaning, she likes neatness. And yet, when Brian comes back, that order falls apart; she can't make this into a neat story. Sharon is grief-stricken but also stuck in her own shame and denial. She's a character who makes slow but instrumental changes.

Travis, Brian's father, cannot accept his son's queerness or that he's dying—and he retreats from Brian and from the family. By only showing Travis through the other characters' eyes, his interiority is inaccessible to the other characters and also to the readers. But he also carries around so much guilt, grief, and loss that he cannot face. I knew that Travis would only get one chance—when it's too late—to speak about his son.

**RG: What are your thoughts on this as a novel of place—to what degree did it have to be set where it is set?**

**CS:** I wanted to write about Appalachian Ohio, a place where my grandparents lived and that still feels like home, partly because I haven't seen it show up much in literature. The setting is rural and isolated, and quite beautiful. Brian wants to see his family, maybe reconcile with them, but he also misses the home where he grew up—the woods behind their house, the hills, the trees.

The time period—1986—is critical to this novel, and in some ways, that's even more crucial than the place. I wanted to examine what was happening outside of urban spaces— how small towns and rural places were grappling with or refusing to face HIV and AIDS. I think this is a story that is Appalachian, and yet a similar story could easily take place in any rural small town in America—in Oregon or Maine or Nebraska.

**RG: You've been a part of various different Appalachian sub-regions. What characterizes Appalachian Ohio in your mind? What distinguishes it from the rest of Appalachia in your mind?**

CS: I'm no expert on Appalachia, but I do think this is a corner of Appalachia that is often overlooked. Southeastern Ohio borders West Virginia, and it's a beautiful area of the state. People tend to think of Ohio as flat land, not hills, and typically assign Appalachia only to settings with coalfields and mountains. And, it's true, Ohio doesn't have mountains like most of Appalachia, but the region has faced similar hardships and suffered at the hands of corporate exploitation and greed—the opioid epidemic, and pollution and toxic waste from strip mining and coal-fired power plants. When I was working on my first novel *The Evening Hour*, I spent a lot of time in the mountains of West Virginia, and much of the place reminded me of southeastern Ohio. The people I met, the culture and language. I hope the novel will be in conversation with other Appalachian novels.

**RG: The film adaptation of *The Evening Hour* premiered at Sundance in January. How did it feel to see your characters and story on the big screen?**

CS: It was amazing. I'm so grateful that I had the opportunity to see the film premiere at Sundance, before the world so drastically changed. To see my characters come to life on the big screen— what a beautiful dream. The director Braden King, screenwriter Elizabeth Palmore, and all the talented actors took great care in capturing the heart and tone of the book, and breathed another life into my story. It took years for everything to come together, and every single person worked extraordinarily hard on this film.

At this point, the film is circulating in film festivals.

**RG: Like many writers with books coming out this spring, your book tour for *The Prettiest Star* was upended by the COVID-19 pandemic. How challenging has this been and how have you adapted?**

CS: In the beginning, it was a major disappointment. I had been looking forward to a book tour that would take me all over the country, and planned to be traveling March through July. So it was very disorienting, as it was for so many of us, when those plans completely fell apart. It was also a strange, slow unraveling. If you remember back in March, which seems like a lifetime ago, most of us didn't grasp the depth or extent of this pandemic. In March, my publishers and I assumed the readings scheduled for May would still go on. Then, in April, we thought surely I'd still be reading in June. Now, I've adjusted and adapted, as most of us have. Though I'd love to socialize and hang out with friends and travel, I'm not planning on doing that for a long time, at least not in a way that doesn't include social distancing and masks. I'm trying to stay healthy and safe, and doing my part to helping others stay safe too.

I'm incredibly grateful for how bookstores and the writing community have adapted during the pandemic—supporting each other, moving readings online, getting the books into readers' hands. It's a testament to how robust the writing community is, and shows how much we need literature and the arts for nourishment and connection. Of course, I miss the physical space of bookstores, but we'll get back there one day. I encourage everyone to keep buying books from independent bookstores so that we can to keep these businesses alive and thriving. ■

# GONE

It is the week after my eldest living aunt has, with us all in proximity, buried her sister.
It is the second sister, out of nine siblings, she has buried. Her youngest brother, gone too.

My Aunt Rosetta, of course, did not lift her eighty-five-year-old, tiny, weathered limbs toward
a shovel, did not plunge it deep into Pennsylvania dirt, did not evict all the tiny

organisms, happily soil-rich and nutrient-drunk, to make room for a concrete vault
cocooning death from spilling into that dark, dank, underground world, in which

a crank, not my aunt's hand, lowered the silver-shellacked box down slowly,
as a cracking voice barely squeaked out the song—*Some glad morning when this life is*

*over, I'll fly away. To a home on God's celestial shore, I'll fly away. I'll fly away, Oh glory,*
*I'll fly away. When I die, Hallelujah, by and by, I'll*—and the singer could not get to flight

a fifth time, her voice clipped by the squawk of a bird soaring overhead, and we looked
up into the lustrous blue staring directly into a sun that swung white, covering

everything in a quick blank flash like a camera capturing us, and not the other way around. My aunt calls this a sign. We are trained to make myths of our losses,

perfume our sadness with the incense of hope. Even ailments serve purpose: A palm itch means money is on the way. Aching bones promise rain will cleanse our debts.

My aunt says her sister, Velma, whose body languished in death, confuised by breath and disinterest in food and drink, nurses with needles, bagged meds and IVs,

was singing back to us, letting us know she been flown the coop of that casket, been knocked on the doors of Heaven and let into its gates, pearled and gleaming, done

met her twin brother born dead in the womb, the one no one speaks of, the one my Aunt Rosetta—sitting at the faux wood kitchen table, near the TV broadcasting Life-

time dramas and ads for white sandy beaches—says she can still see in her mind's eye, how he was not birthed yella and hollering like Velma, but came out without

sound, came the same color blue as his black daddy's eyes. Says she can still remember her Daddy, shuffling around the two-room shack a miner's pay borrowed,

searching for newspaper to wrap all the lack lodging in his still-beating heart, while
he covered his stillborn namesake, carried him away, round the side of the mountain

where men buried coal ash, where he might have hoped the boy renewed his strength,
mounted up with wings like eagles, and took off, singing *I'll fly away. Oh, glory, I'll*

*fly away.* I tell Aunt Rosetta so many of our men have fledged, have not permitted us
the satisfaction of their deaths, have not even left us with a trace of white feathers.

There is no hymn for this. No balm. My father, I tell her, was no bird. He did not crow,
did not flap a brilliant plumage, announcing, as a white flag might,

his defeat. One day, he was just gone. My aunt tries to name all our living losses,
for all we try to seek peace: Her son, once track-star, turned marketer,

turned hospital deserter after another man died beneath his bumper. Another son
who loss language in a hospital bed after another man bat-crushed his head

for stealing his woman without paying. Her grandson whose head was so full
of voices that he forgot his last name, knew only cardboard beneath palm trees near

a beach lined with needles. She tries to name them. *He is* —. She stops. *He was* —.
She stops again. *He would have been* —. We can't sing with certainty about our men.

We don't look up at the sky and see their wings, like Aunt Velma's, cut across clouds.
We won't toss chopped-off rose-heads at their buried beaks. We can't call them—
dead.

**L. RENÉE**

# FISH FRY

Everything delicious is served on Friday.
Jesus should get a do-over for the Last Supper,
since He missed out on the miracle

that is Wonder Bread made paste by perch's
corn-mealed skin sweating Crisco, clinging
like faith to a mouth's roof, even as the tongue

tries to negotiate release, swat freedom for teeth.
We know what delay tastes like.
We have waited for a check that affords us

this feast of fish golden crisp and the glow of black joy.
With Luther Vandross praising us for being bad
on Aunt Mary's 45 spinner, who would call this dinner?

Stove tops bubble with pots of kale and collards
made sides only by smoked ham hock oozing
salty fat, their doneness determined by Mama Joyce

who dips her Too Too Blessed 2 Be Stressed mug in the pot-
liquor and sips slowly, purses her lush lips and declares:
*It got more meldin' to do. Ain't that true for all of us?*

She snorts every time Lil' Russell comes by to kiss her highest
cheekbone, his jeans drifting toward hell like he forgot
his real tribe. *Nevermind, no matter, we made it here together*

the Old Timers will say—though they suck their teeth at the sight
of his drawers, at the sight of a Reneger at their Bid Whist table,
at the scent of Dee Dee's too-sweet macaroni and cheese.

We all fall short of perfection like memory, but Uncle Harold
brings us back to where we started: yellow perch biting their ashen
end of a line in Lake Erie's Ohio waters—the place Grandaddy,

wearing his old mining boots, taught generations the patience
needed to stay fed. Uncle Harold will never bring the tartar sauce
Cousin Cathy, out East, developed a taste for. He will fling back his

James Brown-slicked bouffanted crown and howl the sound of hunting
hounds choking on coal dust, remind her she still a West Virginia holler
girl, remind us travels ain't useful without this knowing.

# TRAPS

## MARY ALICE HOSTETTER

Hap woke up before the alarm went off and switched on the light. He rolled on his side and looked at the framed photo on the bedside table. It was a picture of him with his parents and Valerie, his sister. His aunt Mildred had taken it on Easter a few weeks before his mother died, and they were all dressed up. Dad even wore a tie, probably the last time he had one on, that day and for the funeral.

The photo was torn right above Dad's head, and Hap knew when that tear had happened. It was one day they'd had an argument about Hap using the truck, and Dad had told him it was a good thing his Mama didn't live to see what a poor excuse for a son he'd turned out to be. Hap slammed into his bedroom. Sitting on the bed, looking at the picture, he was so mad he wanted to tear his dad out of it. By the time he'd taken the frame apart and started ripping it down the middle, Hap remembered it was the last picture he had of the whole family, so he taped it up and put it back in the frame. Even with the tape, you could see where it was torn.

Hap got up, dressed and went to the kitchen. He opened the refrigerator to get out the milk. On the refrigerator, held up with a magnet from the hardware store, was a picture of Valerie's baby. She'd sent it with his bus ticket. Over spring break he'd visit her in Kentucky, and see the baby. Having never been around a baby before, Hap didn't know how it would feel to be an uncle, but he was excited about seeing his sister.

When Valerie was living at home, things were better. She kept the house clean and made dinner for them every night. It almost felt like a real home. All three of them sat together to eat. If Dad worked late, Hap and Valerie ate together. In summer she took care of the flower beds and put fresh flowers in a jar in the middle of the table, like Mama. Now he and Dad were on their own, and Hap'd forgotten half the things Valerie had taught him how to cook. The last time he'd tried to make macaroni and cheese, even though it was from a box, he'd done something wrong, and it tasted so bad he had to throw it out. He'd made the cube steak with tomato sauce Valerie had taught him, and thought he'd done it right, but it didn't taste like hers. He was sure she'd ask him what he was eating, and he didn't want to admit most of it came from cans, and sometimes he didn't even heat things up.

He took the cereal out of the rusted metal cabinet, grabbed a mixing bowl from the cupboard over the sink and poured a bowl of corn flakes. He was sitting at the kitchen table eating when he heard Dad coming down the hall from his bedroom. Dad opened the door to the coal stove and slammed it shut.

"Damn lazy kid," he said, "think you're too good to empty the ashes?"

"Wouldn't hurt you to do a little," Hap said.

"You know damn well the doctor said I'm not supposed to strain myself."

"Guess he told you to drink till you pass out too."

"What the doctor says is none of your business. I guess having your Mama dead isn't enough without killing me off too."

Hap shoved his chair so hard it fell over. He kicked it out of his way. He left his bowl on the table, a few corn flakes still floating in the milk on the bottom. Not even taking time to wet his hair and comb down his cowlick, he grabbed his denim jacket and backpack off the hook next to the cupboard and left without saying a word, slamming the kitchen door so hard the loose pane in the window rattled.

It was early for the bus, but he had to get out of the house.

■ ■ ■

Hap was ten when his mother died. The night before, he was already in bed when Dad had come home. He was loud, as usual, yelling at Mama about his supper being cold. Hap hated hearing Dad raise his voice like that. He put the pillow over his head. His head was still halfway under the pillow the next morning.

Hap went out to the kitchen. Dad was there, even though he should have been at the mine by that time. Hap didn't recognize some of the men who were in the house, and Aunt Mildred was there.

Dad looked at him and said, "Hap, your Mama died last night." Aunt Mildred came over and held him. She was sobbing, and Valerie was crying too.

"Poor Esther," Aunt Mildred had said, "she always was so sickly. I'm not surprised pneumonia was enough to take her."

Hap had no idea she was even sick.

■ ■ ■

Hap sat in his sixth period class, slouching in a desk made for someone much shorter. He glanced at the clock on the wall. The hands had not moved far since he looked at it last. Miss Unger was substituting for Coach Wallace, the regular English teacher. She'd retired after teaching almost forty years. She started class by calling roll, as if she didn't know them all. There weren't even a hundred kids in the whole school, including elementary, and she'd taught most of their parents. She'd taught Mama in high school.

Miss Unger picked up a piece of chalk and wrote on the board "What Freedom Means to Me" in handwriting that looked like the alphabet tacked up on the wall in the first and second grade room. She handed out composition paper.

"Since we just celebrated the Bicentennial, I thought this would be a good topic," she said. "It doesn't matter how long your compositions are. Write until you're finished and check back over your papers when you're through. If you have time left, you may read or work on something else."

Hap stared at the blank paper, scrawled his name at the top. Hap. *Short for Happy* is what he always heard. Aunt Mildred said his Mama started calling him that because he was the happiest baby she'd ever seen, and it stuck. He didn't feel that happy. He stared down at his name at the top of the paper, out the window, and again at the clock.

He copied the title on the top of the page. He left space underneath and wrote, "It means I don't have to write this pathetic composition. The End." He checked back over all twelve words, sure he hadn't made any spelling or punctuation mistakes this time, and put his head down on the desk.

The bell rang, and school was over for that day and week. Hap stuffed his notebook and pencil in his backpack, dropped his composition on the desk on the way out and walked toward the bus. It felt wrong not staying for basketball. He walked past clusters of kids talking and laughing, many of them smiling at him, saying "Hi." He was the first to get on the bus; his friend George followed and sat down next to him.

"You deaf?" George said.

"I heard you. Didn't feel like answering."

"Okay. So you're a basketball star, but it doesn't mean you can ignore your friends," George said.

"Have a lot on my mind, that's all," Hap said. "Got nothing to do with you."

"Know what I think? You need a break. Been playing basketball so long you don't know what to do now the season's over."

"I'll be fine without basketball," Hap said.

"We should celebrate. How 'bout we go into town tomorrow night, see a movie, have a couple beers, check out the girls. You're not in training anymore. What can Coach Wallace do? And not like your old man's gonna notice. I'll tell my folks I'm with you. They'll be thrilled."

"Where's the money coming from for this big night?" Hap asked.

"We could take the truck over to the mine tonight, up by the tipple, like last year, and load up clinker coal, mix it with good," George said. "Sell it to somebody who doesn't know any better. Don't get any easier than that, if you ask me."

"Except they have a security guard up at the mine now."

"So? He can only be in one place at a time. And it's not like he's going to shoot us. Those guys don't even carry guns."

"He could make things rough for us if he calls the cops," Hap said. "I don't need that."

The bus had filled around them. It lurched to a start and droned up the hill and down the other side into Tanner's Gap. Half the kids got off at Marshall's Store, the guys pushing in front of each other to get out first to buy sodas and snacks before they walked home. Two girls got off last. Marci smiled at Hap as she went by. Hap knew she liked him, but he wasn't getting involved with Marci or any of the rest. Those giggly girls were so obvious, stopping by his seat on the bus to ask

*The bus had filled around them. It lurched to a start and droned up the hill and down the other side into Tanner's Gap.*

him about math homework or when the next book report was due. Anyone knew he was not the guy to ask about homework. He wasn't rude, but he didn't want to get close to any of them. All up and down the valley were guys who'd gotten stuck, as often as not because they fell for a girl in high school who didn't ever want to move far from home. That wouldn't be Hap.

Frank was on the porch at the store talking to a man Hap didn't recognize.

"Look at Frank, talking to the new preacher," George said. "That'll be the day, Frank goes to church."

The bus went by the post office, where Irene was taking in the flag, and turned right on the county road to go out toward the hollow.

"About getting money?" George said.

"I could try sneaking a few bills out of Dad's wallet, but there's no point. Nothing there," Hap said. "I checked a couple days ago.  A week 'til the next check comes."

"Say we load up the clinker coal, don't take no good coal at all, and sell that," George said. "It's nothing but trash, not like we're taking anything valuable. We can top it off from our coal bins at home. We go over to Hatton's Creek or somewhere people don't know us. They'll never figure out why they can't keep their fire going until someone tells them they're trying to burn black rocks."

"And what if they come looking for us?" Hap said.

"We'll tell them we're sorry. We got cheated. Be an easy forty dollars if you ask me."

"Go ahead if you want to," Hap said. "I don't need to be getting arrested for something stupid."

"You've turned into such a chicken shit. I can't believe you're the same guy who outran three guards over at the prison farm the night we stole those watermelons." George laughed and slapped the back of the seat in front of him.

The bus went around the curve and stopped at the end of the muddy lane that led up to Hap's house.

"See you," Hap said, grabbing his backpack.

"Later," George said.

Hap got off the bus and walked up the lane toward the grey-shingled house that had been his home for his entire life. The walnut tree that went down in the storm a year ago was lying next to the house, and the post with the basketball hoop leaned toward the shed. The day Hap and Dad had put it up, they couldn't find a tape measure ten feet long, so they'd measured a board four feet, and Hap had stood with the board on his head while his dad measured for the hoop. Hap was thirteen then.

After they put the hoop up, Hap practiced every day. If Dad got home before dark, he'd come out and stand under the net as Hap shot one free throw after the other. They dug in a strip of two-by-four to mark the free throw line. Dad kept track of how many shots Hap made in a row. Dad would try to guard him as Hap made a drive to the net. He wasn't very fast, and Hap didn't have much trouble getting by him. Dad would get short of breath and say "I'd better stop. I'm too old for this." He didn't care if Hap got by him and made the shot. When did he start getting angry all the time? Was it after the heart attack, after Valerie left?

The paint around the windows was peeling, and no one did anything about it. Dad tried to take care of Mama's flowerbed the first summer after Valerie left. Now it was grown under, and you couldn't tell it had ever been a flowerbed until daffodils or daisies popped up among the weeds.

Traces of smoke trailed from the chimney. Dad must have gotten the fire going. Hap opened the door to the kitchen. The TV was on, and Dad, lying on the sofa, rolled over and sighed, but didn't wake up. Hap went to the coal bin, filled the bucket and fixed the fire. He took a couple of hot dogs from the refrigerator and put them in a pan of water to boil, opened a can of baked beans and heated them in the dented aluminum pan. He stood at the kitchen counter to eat the beans out of the pan, wrapped the hot dogs in white bread and ate them. When he left, he closed the door carefully behind him. Dad was still asleep on the sofa.

The truck was parked at the top of the lane, the hood unlatched. The last time Hap drove it, the latch came undone, and the hood flapped up. He couldn't see where he was going and almost drove off the road. Didn't want that to happen again. He went into the skinning shed and rummaged through wire and twine, looking for a piece he could use to fasten it.

The late afternoon sun shone through the door and leaked through the cracks between the weathered boards onto the traps hanging on nails along the wall. Hap took down a trap and pressed open the jaws to see if it worked. He tripped the catch with a wooden stake he found on the floor.

■ ■ ■

All those winter mornings ago, Dad woke Hap up to go along to check the traps he'd set down along the creek. Mama had filled the big red thermos with hot chocolate, zipped Hap's coat up to the top, pulled his cap down over his ears and sent him out into the dark with Dad, saying something about "not wanting my trappers to get cold." Hap climbed up into the pickup, and Dad roared off over the frozen ruts, almost bouncing him off the seat.

"Hold on over there, son," Dad had said. "I don't want to lose my partner."

Dad checked the traps, and Hap waited in the truck. If Dad found an animal in one of the traps, usually a muskrat, he brought it back and threw it on the floor under Hap's feet. It landed with a dull thud and made the whole truck smell. If a muskrat was alive in the trap, Dad called, "Bring me my club," and Hap reached behind the seat for the locust branch with the knot on the end that his father used to hit the animals once, hard, and wait for them to stop moving before he took them out of the trap and brought them up to the truck. Hap never watched Dad hit the animals, but he heard the thud and the little yelp they made.

Hap didn't help with the skinning before he went to school, but on weekends he watched Dad do it. Dad knew exactly where to cut to get the skins off, and he tacked them on the side of the shed to dry before he sold them. No skins there anymore, just rusted nails.

Hap found a piece of wire among the twisted tangle of chains and steel. He fastened the hood to the latch, got into the truck and pushed in the clutch. The truck needed a new starter; other than that, it ran fine. He always parked on a hill and coasted it. He'd let out the clutch after it got rolling, and the engine caught, usually on the first try. Lots of hills, so no problem finding places to coast start. There was a time Dad would have been off to the junkyard to find the right starter. He'd have had it fixed in no time.

The road to the cemetery up beyond the church was washed out, but Hap made it with no problem, tires straddling the muddy ruts. At the top of the hill, he swerved the truck around and headed downhill before he cut the engine. With basketball, either practice or games almost every day, he hadn't been to the cemetery in months. He walked down the rows of gravestones, past the tattered flag on the grave of Derwood's son who'd been killed in Vietnam, past the gravestone for Henry, the little boy who was murdered. It was almost like his

*He bent down in front of the stone and cleared away leaves and twigs that had gathered over the winter.*

mother's tombstone was in the row for "people who shouldn't have died." He got to his mother's stone at the end. "Esther Holloway. Loving Mother. Loving Wife. 1939-1969."

He bent down in front of the stone and cleared away leaves and twigs that had gathered over the winter. He picked up branches that had torn off the pine trees, probably in the ice storm, and threw them over the wall at the edge of the cemetery. On the trees, pine sap oozed from where the branches had ripped off. Hap went back to his mother's grave and sat on the cold ground. There wasn't a sound in the cemetery except for the chatter of squirrels. The cold damp chilled him. "Mama," he said, "I wish you'd been there for the final game. Ten seconds left. You should've seen it. The whole town screaming for me, and my shot goes through. Dad didn't feel up to going out, even though Wayne said he'd give him a ride." Hap glanced around.

He picked up a twig lying in the grass, snapped off pieces and tossed them on the ground.

"I gotta leave here."

He wiped tears with the sleeve of his sweat shirt, picked up a short branch and scraped at the muddy ground. Hap stood up and brushed the dirt off the back of his jeans. He coasted the truck until it caught and headed off to the Beer Garden.

■ ■ ■

There were only three trucks in the parking lot, and Wayne's van, of course. Not many for a Friday, but it was still early. On the television up in the corner, Wayne had on the news. They were talking about a new kind of airplane that went so fast it could get to Europe in no time. Landing, it looked like a funny goose. Hap had never been on an airplane, but one day. Maybe not the goose one, but some airplane.

Hap sat at the bar, and Wayne served him a beer without even asking. He wasn't old enough to drink, but Wayne didn't mind, unless there was a customer in the bar he didn't know. If that happened, Wayne'd make a point of asking Hap for his ID, telling him he was sorry, and bringing him a soda. Wayne had to be careful in case the stranger was one of those liquor people. Wayne didn't want to take any chances getting closed down.

A couple of guys from the mill sat at the other end of the bar, and a few more were playing pool. The television gave the room a bluish light.

"I'm still hoarse from all the screaming," Wayne said. "That was one terrific game."

"Thanks," Hap said. "I've never seen that many people in the gym."

"Wasn't easy getting them all there," Wayne said. "I did eight loads in my van, and they picked up the rest in the school bus. When Hawthorne's team saw that crowd, they knew they didn't have a chance."

"They came mighty close," Hap said. "I was lucky on that last shot."

"What about all the rest? They couldn't all be luck."

"Yeah, it was a good game."

"So, the season's over. In a couple months you'll be graduating."

"Can't wait," Hap said.

"Then what?"

"I know I won't be sitting in school in those little desks anymore," Hap said.

"You can't expect they're gonna make desks for guys who are six-four."

"I've done my time."

"So what are you going to do? Washing dishes for me is no kind of career for a guy like you."

"Tell you the truth, I'm thinking about the Marines. Recruiter's coming over next week."

"Marines? You don't like taking the heads off chickens. What are you going to do in the Marines?"

"I'm tougher than you think," Hap said.

"You tell your dad you're thinking about the service?"

"Nah, but he won't care, long as he doesn't have to deal with me anymore."

"Don't be so sure," Wayne said.

"It's not like we're in a war or anything," Hap said.

"But you never know," Wayne said.

Wayne pulled a basket of fries out of the deep fryer, shook them, and propped them to drain. He put some on a plate, salted them and brought them to Hap.

"What about basketball? Just gonna drop that? Coach Wallace was in here last week and said he couldn't imagine ever coaching a player good as you. Said you could get a college scholarship."

"I'm not sure Coach Wallace knows what he's talking about. Not every school's like Patton where any guy over five feet who can walk without tripping himself is gonna start on the basketball team. I'm tall and got lots of playing time, since I was on the team since junior high. Lots of tall people in the world."

"They don't all make all-state."

"I got honorable mention, not first team."

"You would've been first if you had a better team to play with."

"Doesn't matter. I'm through with school."

"You're eighteen," Wayne said, scraping the grill with a spatula and tossing on a couple of hamburger patties. "This is your time to enjoy life."

Hap took a gulp of his beer.

Wayne changed the channel to a basketball game and got busy filling food orders for the guys from the mill. The game was half over when George came in and sat on the stool next to Hap.

"I saw your truck, thought you'd be here. What's the score?"

"Tell you the truth, I have no idea," Hap said.

"What's up with you?" George said.

They sat there for a few minutes, George watching the game, and Hap peeling the label off the beer bottle. Hap slid the empty bottle down the polished wood bar. Wayne grabbed it and brought him another.

The bell on the door jangled, and a couple of miners came in, black dust on their faces and hands. Wayne took their order. Hap finished his beer in a long gulp, slid off the stool and put on his jacket.

"Hold on," George said. "Only five minutes left in the game."

"Let me know how it turns out. Gotta go." Hap said. "Wayne, you can put the beer and fries on my tab."

"Don't worry about it," Wayne said.

Hap coasted the truck until the motor caught, roared the engine. He did a U-turn, bouncing off the edge of the road and back on, and drove home through the darkness.

He parked the truck with the lights shining into the skinning shed. Left the motor running. He pulled out the traps he'd seen earlier and oiled the springs and catches, found the stakes leaning against the wall in the corner. He stuffed the traps and stakes into a burlap bag, threw it in the back of the truck and cut the engine. In the quiet house his dad had already gone to bed.

■ ■ ■

When Hap got up early the next morning, it was cold and dark. He walked out to the kitchen in his stocking feet and heated milk for hot chocolate. He poured it into the old thermos he'd found the night before in the back of the cupboard. All he could find for bait was an apple. Dad always said, "It's a poor trapper has to waste good food to catch a muskrat," but an apple's what there was. He put on his heavy parka, knit cap and boots, picked up the thermos of hot chocolate and a flashlight. He coasted the truck farther than usual before he popped the clutch.

He found a place to park near the stream and took the

traps and stakes from the back of the truck. He walked along the bank looking for a spot to set the first trap. Even with the flashlight, he couldn't see where he was going and almost tripped when his boot caught in a hole. He set the first trap at a bend in the stream, attaching the chain to the stake and pounding it down with a rock. He balanced a piece of apple on the trigger. He went on downstream, setting and baiting all the traps, and had finished the last one when he heard a muffled snap upstream, and a yelp.

Hap walked back, shining his flashlight along the bank at each of the traps until he got to one of the first ones he'd set.

*Even with the flashlight, he couldn't see where he was going and almost tripped when his boot caught in a hole.*

The chain on the trap rattled as the muskrat struggled to get free; Hap shone his flashlight on it thrashing on the muddy bank. The stake held tight. He had only planned to set the traps and check back later. He hadn't brought anything along to use as a club. How could a muskrat get caught so quick? The muskrat showed its teeth and made a clicking sound when Hap moved closer. It was caught by its back leg. He aimed his flashlight up the bank until he found a stick. He came back, propped the flashlight so its beam shone toward the trapped muskrat. It was hard to see with the shadows. The muskrat moved again, snapping at the stick as Hap moved closer. Hap lifted the stick, paused, and brought it down. Holding the flashlight in one hand, he fumbled with the stick until he lined it up to release the trap. He pushed it down as hard as he could, and the trap sank into the mud. Finally the jaws opened, and the muskrat pulled its leg free. It lay there for a minute, slid down the bank into the stream and swam away.

Hap snapped all the traps, gathered them up, tossed them into the back of the truck and drove home. In the rearview mirror, the sky glowed a faint pink. When he got back to the house, he drank the last of the hot chocolate, still warm in the thermos, and went back to bed. He'd have to tell Valerie he went trapping.

Dad had already had breakfast and was rinsing his bowl when Hap went out to the kitchen the next morning.

"Thought I heard the truck in the night. Did you go out?" Dad said.

"I set traps down by the creek."

"What possessed you to do that?"

"Just felt like it."

"Catch anything?"

"Yeah. One. I let it go."

"Probably just as well. Doubt you can sell those skins anymore."

"I wondered."

"Traps still work? Thought they might be rusted too bad."

"I oiled them. They work fine."

"Can't believe it. You taking up trapping."

"Don't think I'll do it again," Hap dumped corn flakes into the bowl and added milk.

"So, you around today?" Dad asked.

"Thought I'd call Harley and see if I could borrow his saw to cut up the tree out back," Hap said. "Try to sell the wood. Should be dried out by now, long as it's been down."

"That's a lot to do, all that wood. Not sure I can be much help."

"Don't worry about it. George'll help me. I'll pick him up when I get the saw."

■ ■ ■

Hap and George cut two loads of firewood, sold them to the young couple moving in at the Lentz place. Dad helped load the smaller pieces and watched from the porch. He said the place looked a lot better without that ugly tree next to the house. They burned the brush and roasted hot dogs when the flames died down, Dad too. They sat on stumps, the three of them, by the dying fire. Hap had left the light on in the kitchen when he went in to get the mustard and ketchup. With the warm light shining through the windows, it almost looked like a home. ■

# ON BIRDS

Appearing in the blush threads of morning
or deep in the indigo hours, alone,
or gaggled in the damp ryegrass—

sometimes humming among
the thrashed wheat, a few chestnut-banded,

others with naked vermillion heads,
the impossibility of their bodies
carried on graceless primitive legs.

Below the sugar maples, robins.
Descendants of one who'd plucked
a thorn from the temple of the dying Christ,

while sparrows scuttled and whistled
at the feet of Romans and the unbaptized.

What of starlings, the interminable
pitchy chorus? Souls of suicides perhaps
as they purr and rattle low in the cedars,

I think, in purgatory there are only black birds,
their stygian wings pressing into
the backs of the penitent.

In Heaven, peacocks.
Resplendent and, according to the Greeks,
incapable of decay.

Unlike Levis's wren in the gravel
flushed with lice and emptiness—

In truth there is no parable,
even in the instant when hundreds of ordinary
small birds thrust their wings against the air

and the whole history of empire-building,
high rhetoric, scientific invention
gives way in the fervor of their strokes.

This is what is meant by *divine*. This,
and the little blood-fat mites riddling
the feathers, each a kind of god,

carried on the head
of a white-breasted nuthatch
skittering across the limbs of apple trees.

**JAE DYCHE**

# ELEGY AS A RAILROAD WATCH

The watch—gifted to my grandfather
(or great-grandfather?) from the B&O Rail Company,

token for his service; the hours, I'm told,
spent between his fiddle and whiskey—

its black hands resting at exaggerated numerals,
5:56 and thirty seconds; have for some time,

though I couldn't say for how long;
or his name; or the angle of his jaw,

the lines beneath his eyes; whether his stubble glinted
the same auburn as my father's—

all I know is he was a *railroader*,
of the many chafed and bent; hammering spikes

into Appalachian bedrock—
and Appalachia is unforgiving place.

Yet someone had to lay the rails;
hitch America with pins and girders, corroded

relics of industry and the engine; of the new world.
When father's people settled here, the mountains

were *frontier* or *Allegheny*—
or *fine river*; before the Potomac flushed with rust

left by generations of freight cars ferrying coal
from our hills to Cleveland, Detroit, Chicago;

to power another man's machines,
soot etched to the row homes and fellowship halls

staggering towards the Potomac's metallic depths:
Piedmont, Cumberland, Martinsburg,

cracked mortar and ocher ghosts.
Nonetheless, except a finger-worn crescent

 on the back, the watch is polished; kept
in a silk pocket envelope in father's bureau;

in mine now:
and I don't want it to be there—

what do I know of granite and iron-straps, or scabs;
of a day's hard labor, the weight of the sledge;

the dialects of oak and creosote.
Of 5:56 and thirty seconds. Of the steady outlying

host of whistles; smut collecting in the brick,
around puddles and porch steps,

my father's tennis shoes wet and loose. What do I know
of Salvation Army clothing; of *to provide for*.

Of his blotched shoulders; or brow against a window
of the coach car, morning fog gathering,

unspent seconds on the glass.
What could I know of the sage cotton curtain

drawn across the hospital room;
of the whole of a man's parts

set onto legal paper and notarized:
bone and blood; ore and hot slag,

the space of the train car bench
between father and daughter;

Mid-Western bethels of steel and exhaust;
my father lost in the syllables

of great named trains: *Empire Builder, City of New Orleans,
California Zephyr,* syllables trembling and lurching

forward beyond abeyance;
beyond the Allegheny Front and Cumberland Valley;

further than Pittsburg smokestacks and Ohio River;
into the open expanse of memory.

**JAE DYCHE**

# AXIS MUNDI

At the center of gravity's pull
is a kitchen table, chipped laminate

at the corners, dusted in whole-meal flour,
skitters of biscuit dough, a gaggle

of bank pens and plastic spice shakers;
Sunday suppers, Grandfather's chair closest

to the door, his ubiquitous tin of peaches,
a golden-syruped jewel

wobbling on the fork prongs, towards
his fleshy wet gums; bread and butter

set out at eleven, replaced by brown gravy
at 5:30. Sunday dinners, heads bowed

as we *bless this food for our use and us*
*for yours*, and the universe slows

to a more manageable pace
of local gossip, the neighbor's daughter-in-law

and last week's doctor appointments, of baked ham
and scalloped potatoes, of the bowl of applesauce,

of a woman in the early morning, sipping
coffee with milk, alone with plain-hearted thanks.

**JAE DYCHE**

# MILK

**VANESSA VAN BESIEN**

B ean kicked the habit seven times, and when she pulled up the two-mile dusty drive of the McCullough ranch, the habit kicked back in as it always had. When her parents didn't want to deal with their rebellious daughter, they sent her away to her grandparents' farm in Scots-heavy western Pennsylvania. Bean had always behaved there, thinking herself a burden whenever she had been dropped on their porch. Her parents were still children themselves, and the punishment they inflicted was a thinly veiled desire for a vacation from their own responsibilities. She was an adult now, and sought this punishment of her grandparents' attention. This was the only bridge she had yet to burn. She brushed past the big-boned woman propped against the paint-chipped wraparound porch.

"And how are we today, other than skinny?" Grandma Maggie asked.

"Good. Great," she lied, and leaned in for a hug. Maggie wrapped her arm all the way around Bean, gripping her ribcage with her large hands.

"Long drive, Grandma. I'm gonna freshen up in the bathroom," Bean said.

Maggie knew the dance and played along, having started to make lunch. Bean found comfort in the routine of the ranch. It'd been five years since she walked the juniper shrub-lined drive, and her guilt in being back made her feel her Presbyterian kin could smell the sins amassed in those five years. It had been twelve hours since her last hit, but the sweat rings on her t-shirt could easily be on account of the heat of the August day.

Grandma Maggie scooted a bowl of blueberries and oatmeal past a highchair, and then realizing her mistake, pushed it toward her emaciated granddaughter, no longer an infant. The dementia hadn't completely taken her yet, and her fumbles were more amusing, and not such that the confusion had yet to become a danger. That would come later when she left the cooker on; when Bean switched it off, careful not to make the old, treasure of a woman feel foolish. And it would come later when the owner of a neighboring farm drove by to see her one February blizzard, dressed in nothing but a nightdress. She had been dancing in front of the barn with an imaginary partner.

"I'd have some milk for ya, but you haven't done it yet," she said far behind her cataracts, eyes wide to let in more light. "Doris has probably started squeezing her own for relief, poor girl."

Bean understood the subtle hint and hoisted the same metal jug that hung from the cocked nail under the dinner bell, reminding all who milked what the work was for. Hunger was foreign to her now, replaced with sick. She swung the empty pail and her weightless body down to the barn. Doris was waiting by the rope that Bean would wrap around her neck. Bean lubed her hands and pulled up the stool that had once boosted her to see the wash sink. She wrapped her thumb and forefinger around the teat and pulled, squeezing quickly, using an improvised technique her grandfather had shown her as a very small girl, using compression but not sliding her hands which could irritate Doris. It would take half the time if she used both hands, but she liked to pat Doris with the other hand and catch up, like a family doctor. She was awkward and out of practice. But she craved to be good at something innocent. After the five teats were expressed Doris flicked her tail in relief and turned away from the tin, letting Bean know the job was done. She untied the girl and was careful to disinfect the tender udder.

Bean's labor was heavy up the hill, and she was hungry. She took the now cold bowl of oatmeal from the kitchen table and joined Maggie in silence on the porch. Out in the yard, between the barn and the house was a long pole intended to hang a laundry line. The same heat-tired hound dog tied to it as her childhood, but the dog was younger, as though he had aged in reverse. He only lifted his head for the dinner bell or to inspect the chicks that dared to skirt his pole. He had no purpose since grandpa put down his hunting rifle for good.

Rusted license plates and farm tools welded together in the shapes of animals lined the chipped boards of the house's face.

A shadow box hung high above a window encased worn jazz records her grandfather had played to their exhaustion, owls made from tree bark and flat river stones, and a collection of pipes that seemed to chronicle the maturation of their smoker, the handmade corn cob pipe of a teen farm boy to the briarwood and yellow Bakelite pipe of an executive. She imagined someday her family assembling a macabre shadow box dedicated to her, featuring the maturation of a heroin user. Baby spoons and ornamental spoons. Spoons willed to her from grandparents, all bent and blackened. Bean stood on tiptoes and tried to flick the corncob pipe into her opposite hand, fumbling with it until it crashed to the ground scattering kernels and stale tobacco across the porch.

"Goddamn it!" said Bean, regretting her word choice immediately.

"Now, I don't know where you've been, girl, and frankly I don't think I wanna know. But you don't ever use the Lord's name in vain in this house. You're too old for the soap, but you can spend the night out here with Horace until you learn more

*The sweat had been dry long enough that she could feel the urge again. The need hit hardest when she was alone.*

appropriate ways to talk," said Maggie, heading for the door, pointing her cane at the laundry pole, and letting the screen slam behind her.

She lay down, back to the splintered boards of the porch, somehow relishing being held accountable for her words and actions. The sweat had been dry long enough that she could feel the urge again. The need hit hardest when she was alone. She recalled being abandoned on a doorstep as she was so often as a child. But the warm smell of bannock baking for the morning met her nose, and it was enough for her now. Bean fell asleep before her Newport Menthol could reach the filter.

The sun beat down on her face just a moment before the rooster could tell her it was morning. The combination of sight and sound made Bean feel her punishment was complete and she assumed she could get an hour of sleep in a bed before Grandma Maggie was up. She shuffled her feet firmly over the boards that would creak if she lifted them to take a step and avoided the exposed nail heads that a child remembers to map out after stubbing a toe painfully, blood running across the floorboards and the loss of a toenail, the regrown nail never quite right. It grew up, and not forward, and wore holes in her shoes.

Bean let too much weight fall on her left foot, and the board caused a door to creak open as if she had stepped on a secret lever. It was the first room in the house to feel the sun, and the bleached sheets of the twin bed illuminated the bleached walls and the bleached furniture, stripped of any bacteria, perceived and real, or anything living at all. The family Bible was particularly dark in contrast, hanging over the edge of the bedside table as though it were asking to be picked up, so obvious in place and color. It was in the same spot she remembered seeing it that day she was fifteen, and life was last present.

The faint smell of pipe tobacco still clung to the fabric curtains. Now there was no hum from the oxygen tank. There was no black stream running from his lips, down his cheek, and onto his pillow. Clouds enveloped the sun and dimmed the room in dappled grey and navy. Bean widened her eyes in an attempt to let in more light, but she itched and all she could see clearly was her bruised arms pocked like a white pointillistic tattoo.

Bean heard a shuffling from her grandma's room across the hall and ran for her bag, closing the bathroom door behind her, the latch clanging but not locking. She flipped on the faucet and set up her kit. All her instruments were concealed in a gutted copy of Judith Guest's *Ordinary People*, a gift from her professor when he discovered she wouldn't be returning in the fall. Orange caps, insulin needles, the medical blue of the tourniquet, the tiny fibrous cloud of the torn Q-tip. Her keys held the metal capsule that held her relief.

She looked up at the mirror. Her license said she was twenty-years-old, 150 pounds, an organ donor, and blonde with blue eyes. A grey film covered her skin and hair, and her shoulders were just wide enough to keep her V-neck from falling to the floor. She was a universal donor who wouldn't be able to donate again, no matter how many years clean, no matter the healthy pink that would be returned to her skin, or the brightness that would be restored to her eyes. She emptied the majority of the capsule on her spoon, more white than usual, and the short rig spit enough water to mix a thick draw. She didn't bother to burn out the impurities. She wrapped the tourniquet around her less-bruised right arm.

Bean felt herself flushed with relief at seeing the syringe cloud red as she coaxed the plunger back with her teeth and then felt greater relief as she pushed the warm rust into her puckered vein. Even EMTs had to prod her pallid, pincushion arms, finally accepting defeat and drawing blood through her wrist. Bean could hit the vein on an orange. A *Farmer's Almanac* dangled by yarn in front of the pull-chain cistern toilet. She squeezed an alcohol pad in the crook of her arm, a sobering moment just now, flashing at her, she thinking her grandpa could see her. He was dead, and she was an atheist, but if God were anywhere he would be in this house. She recalled how when she was sick with the flu as little girl her grandmother, standing just outside the bathroom, wet rag in hand had said, "You throw up like your grandpa; from your feet to the top of your head!" Bean hadn't known what she meant. She heaved her empty stomach into the bowl of the toilet, and with it the weight of her limbs and memory of her grandpa's face as he died. Bean found God in that moment and clutched at the dangling *Farmer's Almanac* like a holy rosary, until her head fell backward through the shower, the curtain collecting around her like a halo, and welcomed the blackness.

She awoke in the gleaming white room, the brightness strangling her pounding head, and it made her cry out in choking sobs.

Grandma Maggie rushed in at the sound of her. She couldn't have been further than the hallway. "Welcome back. I was about to have Father O'Malley come by to read your last rites."

Grandma Maggie had often referred to the fictitious Father O'Malley, and often used in addition to or in place of, "Jesus, Mary, and Joseph!"

Bean said nothing, or maybe she didn't.

"Did you mess in your bed? You must be thirsty. I'll get some water."

Her hips throbbed, and she felt too tired to sit up, or maybe she couldn't. Maggie lifted the water to Bean's chapped lips, but Bean was only able to take it in small sips.

"Do you remember this morning?" Maggie asked.

"In the bathroom?" asked Bean.

"No, that was three days ago. This morning you sat up in bed as you're doing now and asked me where you were. At least you know who I am now."

Bean's bladder woke up angry. She threw the blankets off of herself and was surprised that she had not, in fact, messed in her bed after three days. Maggie had dressed her in a matching cotton pajama shirt and pants with a cheerful, sunflower scatter print design. Her fingernails were trimmed, cleaned to the point of residual painfulness, and then painted pale pink. Bean pushed her legs off the bed onto the floor, but they wouldn't carry her. She willed her muscles to bear the weight, but her urge was too strong, and Maggie watched as she army-crawled to the bathroom, dragging her useless legs behind her like a lame dog her grandpa would've shot.

The bathroom was scrubbed and disinfected of the incident, and her shower curtain halo had been replaced. The new shower curtain featured a giant cherub with rosy cheeks, strumming a harp. Bean dragged herself to the cistern toilet and used her hands to position herself just so, as though mounting a pommel horse the way she had in gymnastics class. She had to spread herself with her fingers to break whatever blockage prevented her piss from flowing. It hurt the more she pissed, and when she wiped she realized her clitoris was the blackest shade of purple and three times bigger than she remembered. She ran cool water on a wad of toilet paper, and pressed it to her crotch, but the water felt warm as though she had used the wrong handle. This would be more of a loss to her than use of her legs, she thought, surprising herself that such a thing could matter just now.

Bean dropped to the ground so she could pull her pants up and dragged herself back to the white room, unable to maneuver around the nail heads. Grandma Maggie hoisted her ragdoll of a granddaughter onto the white twin bed. The farm work kept her strong for a woman in her seventies. Bean guzzled the water at her bedside, exhausted from her trip, and it spilled from the corners of her mouth onto the pillow. She put the glass down on the end table and stared down at her nails. The skin on her hands was peeling and looked as though it was pulling away from her fingertips. Maggie pulled the curtains open and let in the gin smell of the juniper shrubs outside the window.

"I'm sorry, Grandma. I won't take His name in vain again," It was all she could think to say.

"That's enough, Bean. You're still here. You've been blessed with more time to apologize to Him. More time for a lot of things..."

Bean felt guilty, seeing her grandmother, never comfortable showing too much sweetness or too many tears, look as close to crying as she had ever seen.

"Why didn't you call the cops? I mean, why did you take care of me?"

"You don't beat a dog for being sick and no one knows better than me how to take care of my girl. And your grandpa would've agreed. Don't need to be saying *yes sir, no sir* on my own ranch."

She should have a record a mile long by now, but she was somehow always protected from that reality. Maggie carried a galvanized metal wash bin into the room, warm, sweet floral-smelling suds sloshing over the handles, and placed it on the ground next to the white bed.

"I'm gonna have you hang off the side so I can wash that hair. Don't want your curls to dread any more than they already have against that pillow."

As Maggie dragged her thick fingers through her granddaughter's knotted hair, Bean was embarrassed. She imagined taking care of her grandma this way, especially after her fifteenth summer. It seemed inevitable to her. And this made her feel silly, like an invalid. Her grandpa managed to shower himself up until the day he died, not even requiring the use of the shower stool he had put together the day before. But Maggie treated Bean as when she had the flu so many years ago. Her generation had a hard time talking about pain they couldn't see. When Bean's grandpa died, she understood the black fluid trailing from his lips was a result of something rupturing, but she always imagined that it was his anger or the bad that everyone has. She never saw him angry, at least for nothing greater than his Basset mix absconding with a loaf of bread from the counter and then ingesting the entire loaf, leaving the undamaged wrapper the only evidence. But he must have felt real anger at times. She knew it had to be there. She thought it remarkable that her grandpa had such capacity for kindness and not flying off the handle all the way to the end. Maggie squeezed the water out of Bean's hair and wrapped it in a not-as-tight as usual braid.

Maggie brought Bean her grandpa's walking cane. The handle was a swan, flat-backed and humble, lighter where her grandpa's hand had rested. It allowed her to walk to the kitchen, but only if her other hand could press against the walls as she went along. Once she made it to the kitchen, she regained her strength and made it the ten extra feet to the porch. Her muscles had atrophied from her body lying stone still for three days. Her hips were like the Tin Man's, forgotten in the forest and rusted. She hadn't forgotten the painful purple bud between her legs, but the excitement of living through the overdose was over and now she was left with the sick. She dropped herself onto the rocking chair where she

*The days without nourishment beat out the withdrawal nausea and she devoured the meal in minutes, her breath more food than air.*

used to swing her legs while the grown-ups sat inside during holiday meals. Now Maggie preferred meals on the porch in summer while she could, feeling the breeze, and reminder she was still here. The expansive barn bench in her kitchen seemed to highlight the empty spaces.

Bean knew what her grandma had made before she had sat the plate down in front of her. There was apple in those sausages, and butter made from the milk she collected. She could even smell the acid of the tomato. The days without nourishment beat out the withdrawal nausea and she devoured the meal in minutes, her breath more food than air. She sat for twenty minutes willing herself to put her plate in the sink. It was one of her grandmother's many rules.

"Grandma, why would you let me stay here instead of sending me back to school like mom wanted?"

Maggie tossed a couple of pieces of bannock on Bean's plate to sop up the gravy. It was from the night spent on the porch, and stale, but it comforted her to know she hadn't missed out on the simple, but delicious bread.

"I don't obey my children. I also don't think school is best for a young woman such as yourself. Read a book if you want to, them's good. Girls now spend so much time proving they can do it on their own. But who cares? No sense in making life harder for yourself," she looked to the dog, unchained at her feet. "Grandpa and I got twice the living done."

"Maybe you're right." It sounded simple. "Too much excitement for one day. I think I should get some sleep."

The warmth of the evening sun on her skin and the apple sausage in her stomach radiated down to her hips and took an edge off the pain. Bean was relieved that she wouldn't be able to do much for herself. When left to her own decisions she tended to do things like overdose in her grandmother's bathroom.

Bean gained enough strength to lift herself up and cane her way to the sink. She didn't have to balance herself against the wall this time. She hobbled a few steps but stood at the edge of the hallway in her sunflower pajamas and thought hugging her grandma wouldn't be enough, so she did nothing. She turned and went back down the hallway to the white room.

At midnight she had been asleep for five sweaty hours, but her stomach woke her up, and leaned over the side of the bed in time to land her vomit into the shampoo wash bin. She coughed and vomited again. She wiped her mouth with her hair towel and rinsed with the fresh water glass Maggie left on the table. This would be her life for the next two weeks. Last time she quit it took three to stop the vomiting, she thought. She had never quit long enough to rid herself of the itch. She was convinced it wasn't possible. Bean had an awful thought. She remembered the backup foil of dope she kept in a Neil Sedaka CD in her center console. The walk to the car didn't seem as far as the walk to the kitchen had been earlier.

She knocked the swan across the floor out of her reach and hid her hands under the white sheets, sitting on them until they hurt, nails to a cross. In Sunday school, Bean often had to sit on her left hand while she wrote or colored, so she wouldn't write with the devil's hand as she was often reprimanded from doing. She licked her hand and moved it over her sunflowers, opting for the lesser of two evils. She massaged her clitoris and it didn't feel good and she cried, but she continued. She poured the cold water over it to see if she could feel the shock. She rubbed harder and changed directions as if learning her body for the first time. After an hour her orgasm broke through the pain and she came quietly with her mouth open and her eyes closed. It was a reaction her boyfriends always took personally because she grew quieter the better it felt, and where was the validation in that? But it wasn't about them. She cried harder knowing her pleasure wasn't gone but felt that desire as dangerous to her as her ability to walk.

Bean woke up the next day to a bright and cool September. She regained a piece of herself the night before, recognizing she had been starving. She swung her legs to the side of the bed and sighed at the cane she had thrown out of her reach. She stood, steadying herself on the end table, let go, and was on both feet for the first time in days. She walked past the cane and slid her hands across the hallway wall as she made her way to the dining bench in the kitchen.

Maggie was eating breakfast at the table.

"It's too cold out there for September," she said. "*Almanac* saw it coming."

Bean thought it was because the table seemed less lonely with someone to cook for who ate more than scraps, as Horace did.

"I'm feeling much better today, Grandma," said Bean. "I'm thinking it would be smart to bring in some firewood and collect kindling before we need it."

"Oh, yes. Get those muscles moving. You're more useful to the devil when your hands are idle. I could use a fire tonight."

Bean smiled a private smile, ate her eggs and bacon and tomato and went to find her purse. Maggie had set it out on the porch as she did with things that got sprayed by skunks. She had also taken anything that looked to a woman in her seventies that one could use to get high. This included her Tic-Tacs. She found her keys and headed down to the car. Her movements were slow but more fluid now, more oil can into her Tin Man. After unlocking the rusty car with a key in the door handle, the smell of her car and her life before the ranch was overpowering. Cheetos and menthol cigarettes and musty clothing. She flipped through the center console and found the sixties pop record and flipped the wrapped foil into her palm and slipped it in her pocket.

As she walked back up the drive she stopped at every juniper bush and tore off the brittle needles under branches that would burn easily. The pine smell and the breeze she felt filled her with an energy, and though weak, she was powerful. When Bean reached the porch Maggie yelled from the kitchen.

"You've got more milking to do tomorrow. That batch has already turned from the heat."

Bean looked into the yellow jug, at the attempt of her old self, and set down her branches. She pulled the foil out of her pocket and opened it over the container. The powder was absorbed immediately, and Bean's heart beat hard against her chest. She wanted to cry or laugh or shoot up or yell. Instead she picked up a rick of wood from the shed and regathered her dried shrubs.

After dinner Bean took her copy of *As I Lay Dying* out of the car, this one not scooped out for drug purposes, and let the urges come and go. Maggie joined her with the *Almanac*.

She piled the logs in the fireplace. Bean lit the sawdust bed under the kindling she gathered from the parched juniper bushes that scaled the yard. Above the fireplace was the framed cross-stitch she made her grandmother at Sunday school. Rust-colored flowers circled the words, "Burning, not yet consumed." ■

# MATCH GIRL

We were all young once—
Hair the texture of corn silk,
Thighs as tight as melons,
Eyes that danced fire,
Hearts that hummed rock anthems

Until it melted away—
Diaphanous at first,
Mist spiralling from dry ice,
Then faster like wax melting
Beneath a blue flame, layer upon

Layers of carefully dipped wax
Shearing away until nothing
Is left but the fume of smoke,
Breathed in and held tightly
In the lungs of a generation newly lit—

Blowing out, the scent of sulphur
Limning our entire arc of existence

**LISA M. KENDRICK**

# JAWBREAKER

Flipping his blond hair to one side,
his blue eyes dismissed your resolve.

You learned about his sugar cravings
the same way everyone else does—

how he goes through relationships
never savoring the slick flavor

or swallowing the tartness slowly
like most do with a cherry Jolly Rancher.

Instead, his dexterous fingers
pry chocolate kisses from back seats.

He pops them between his full lips,
half-melted Hershey candy,

his tongue shoving it down his throat
while wiping his hands on his jeans.

You know now how he devours people,
how everyone learns the hard way with him.

But you still savor the fantasy
that one day he will slip up

and snatch a Gobstopper—jaw cracking,
teeth breaking, and impossible to swallow.

**LISA M. KENDRICK**

# LEAVING THE MOUNTAINS
## PASSING SPRINGFIELD, MA ON I-91

Half-moon hugs
it's knees above
a parking garage.
It's just a broken cookie
in a halo of spilt milk
during the sour end
of a late night drive.
Mountains refuse
to follow me here.
Fatigue fakes reason—
it's speeding-taillight
gut-punch-pulsing
through memory.
Night leans heavy,
triggers the city's horns—
I imagine casino goers
tapping chipped
glitter-nails on leather
steering wheel covers
and swearing behind
their tinted windows.
My hope bleeds openly,
ripped cuticles and
missed exits I haven't
painted over in years.
Destinations not worth
turning around for
unless there's nowhere
else to go home to.

**ALISON TERJEK**

# BOOK REVIEWS

Aaron Smith. *The Book of Daniel*. Pittsburgh, Pa.:
University of Pittsburgh Press, 2019. 108 pages. Softcover.
$17.00.

*Reviewed by Savannah Sipple*

To some readers, Aaron Smith's
newest poetry collection *The Book of
Daniel* might read like an homage to
pop culture, poetry, and gay icons,
but these poems ache with lust,
anger, desire, grief, and sex, and they
offer no apologies for not being able
to reconcile the ways those things
coexist.

Smith writes about our culture's
fascination with celebrity by weaving
together names familiar in both pop
culture and the literary world. In the poem "Celebrity," he says:

*Anne Sexton died in 1974, the year I was born.*
*Thomas James died in 1974 and was born*
*in Joliet, Illinois, where I was born. He wrote*
*Letters to a Stranger before he killed himself.*
*I've written three books few people read*
*and wanted to kill myself.*

[and later]

*....I went*
*to the building in SoHo where Heath Ledger died.*
*Flowers on the sidewalk, body bag dragged out*
*under camera flash. I tried to explain to engineers*
*I worked for why his death was a big deal, but they were*
*homophobic and incapable of nonlinear thinking.*

Literary and cultural icons carry the same significance for Smith, and this poem sets the tone for the entire collection. First, it captures the way we often try to make personal connections with those we idolize. We could be them:

*Todd Haynes took a blade to Barbie's*
*face to make it look like Karen Carpenter lost weight.*
*Basquiat and Winehouse were 27, too. If the elevator tries*
*to bring you down. If pills plus alcohol plus fame, then*
*the answer must be River Phoenix. Go crazy.*

The rest of the collection holds nothing back in the way it tackles complexities of being gay, having a deeply religious upbringing, and fighting to simply exist.

It's hard to choose whether Smith's honesty is the sharpest in regard to grief or desire. The title poem of the collection "The Book of Daniel" is not, in fact, a retelling of the Biblical lion's den, but is a litany of desire about Daniel Craig. It uses the *modus operandi* of a serial killer to capture his obsession:

*I fell in love with Daniel Craig*
*when he was stalked by a man in Enduring Love—*
*before he was Bond-hot and too famous. I fantasize how*
*I could kidnap the guy from the gym whose nipples*
*slip out of his Red Sox tank top. He acts like it's okay*
*to love his body. I could use chloroform or a gun*
*to take him. I'm not sure what to do after that,*
*but I eat hard candy in bed and imagine it.*

We associate serial killers with violence because if we associate them with desire, then don't we all have the potential to cross that line? And where does the line begin: with a scrapbook, a journal, a lock of hair? Does it start with a stare at the gym, a sweet in the mouth? In all of this winding of desire and obsession and violence, Smith drops a subtle line in "He acts like it's okay / to love his body," and there the duality deepens. Which does the speaker desire more: the guy from the gym or his confidence? Do we want to be celebrities, or do we want to be with them?

We hold multitudes of beings within ourselves and this is what makes our relationships complex and sometimes painful, particularly for queer folks whose parents tell us to "get AIDS and die," as noted in Smith's "The Dancing Lesbian." It feels like the mother-son relationship has moved past this painful moment, but it captures the ways in which contrasting emotions can exist at once. Because of this, it seems fitting that interspersed with desire, *The Book of Daniel* also captures the grief of a parent's cancer diagnosis; the presence of one emotion doesn't negate the other. These poems cut close to the bone in the way they quietly portray the mother/son relationship. "Diagnosis" compares receiving the news to the time his father hit a deer, and in "Living" we see the mother at her most vulnerable admit "I love my house / and my stuff, I'm so afraid of dying—". But in "Things I Could Never Tell My Mother," the speaker admits he once wrote a poem with that title full of the things that might have upset his mother, but now he writes:

> ...*Things*
> *I haven't told my*
> *mother: Get better.*
> *I don't know who*
> *I'll be after you die.*

What does our narrative become once someone we've been so anchored to is no longer there? What remains?

If there is one area where I wanted more from this book, it was an even deeper exploration of the connective tissue of pain between grief and desire. Both hurt. One of Smith's greatest strengths is his ability to examine some of our most intimate and innate emotions, as well as their malleability. They shift and change over time, and it seems the author has more to say.

In *The Book of Daniel*, Smith pushes us toward this moment of catharsis—not just of grief, but also of lust—one where the man is able to exist without being followed by the word *faggot* or by his own anger or shame, one where he finally finds his happiness. But the moment doesn't come, and the speaker gives in to the notion it may likely never arrive. Perhaps relief does not exist. But if it doesn't, he says, "I just want to walk through my life unarmed." That shouldn't be too much for anyone to ask for.

Matthew Ferrence. *Appalachia North*. Morgantown, W.Va.: West Virginia University Press, 2019. 274 pages. Softcover. $26.99.

*Reviewed by Emily Masters*

Water is the current carrying Matthew Ferrence along the map of his life in his memoir *Appalachia North*. From the water in our streams to the water in our ponds to the water in the blood running through our veins, he traces his life through the moments of transition and movement visible in water. When he moves away from his home in southern Pennsylvania, what he

misses most is the water constantly shaping the landscape. As a child, he spent his time playing in the streams at the bottom of his parent's farm, and as an adult, he recognizes how politicized his known landscapes are by corporate resource ownership and lack of respect for the environment, especially when it comes to damaging water sources. He explores shifting landscapes, questions ownership, and asks what it means when the maps we have of our bodily landscapes are shaken to the core.

In a world where Appalachia is a place of fluctuating borders, Ferrence extends his definition of Appalachia all the way up through the eroded ranges of Canada, what he calls "Canappalachia." While this may irk some readers, especially those with a narrow view of what defines Appalachia, it is powerful to hear the perspective of someone who is from the often-overlooked northern Appalachia. He argues for a continuation of the definition based on landscape—on the connection drawn by lines of the long-standing, long-eroded Appalachian mountain range, and he questions powers that be who define maps for and profit from some of the nation's poorest areas and people.

The environmental bent of *Appalachia North* is a powerful one. From the beginning, Ferrence emphasizes how from an early age he has been conscious of industrial destruction of the environment. From water pollution to issues of returning a mountain to contour to destruction of private property for mineral rights, he is outspoken about his desire for the landscape he has known since childhood to remain stable. He's disappointed, however, when he returns to his family's farm to find gas wells marked with wooden stakes across the property. In a moment of empowerment, he uproots one and hurls it across the field, one small act of rebellion speaking volumes.

As I read Ferrence's memoir, I found myself drawn to his constant need to redefine: our bodies, our identities, our maps. He writes of tension in self-identification growing up in a place technically within the Appalachian Regional Commission defined territory of the region in Pennsylvania, but both inside and outside of what he sees as the typical Appalachian experience. He doesn't discover his Appalachian-ness until attending college in West Virginia. As someone who had never thought of myself as Appalachian until college, his questioning of and redefining identity rings true.

While it is clear Ferrence is winding together tributaries of defining what Appalachia means to him and what a brain cancer diagnosis does to his sense of self, the latter thread is often lost, turning more into a trickle than a stream, and resurfacing when it is least expected and sometimes nearly forgotten. I expected more emphasis on what seems like such a pillar of how Ferrence defines his relationship to the world around him. More focus on the emotional side of his story would have been welcomed in a memoir sometimes bogged down in fact and research above emotional plight.

The academic tone Ferrence takes on is most evident in his eighth chapter "Reading Like an Appalachian." He takes it upon himself to review books set in and near his hometown, tearing apart what he feels like does not do his place justice. The chapter feels misplaced, like it would sit more at home in a magazine or journal than in his memoir. That said, the entirety of his memoir is well-researched, and Ferrence makes sure to support every claim he makes about how he is defining Appalachia and himself.

"I am as I am mapped," Ferrence shares, as he explores how his sense of place and of self is shaken when he is diagnosed with brain cancer. In *Appalachia North*, he takes control over how he is mapped, wresting his map from MRI results and from gas companies, from the ARC definition of Appalachia and from doctor's offices.

He also writes, "Maps can and must be redrawn." It is key for all of us to question how we are mapped and who does the mapping, to constantly redraw, rework, and redefine our maps until we uncover a space that feels like home, like a river carving a landscape to find its best fit.


**Molly Dektar. *The Ash Family*. New York, N.Y.: Simon and Schuster, 2019. 342 pages. Hardcover. $26.00.**

*Reviewed by Donna M. Crow*


With the determination and perseverance of a frontier scout, Molly Dektar wields a sword of truth that delivers a fierce exploration of humankind's place in the diminishing landscape of nature. But it is with the precision and patience of a surgeon's scalpel that she surveys the nuances of the human psyche.

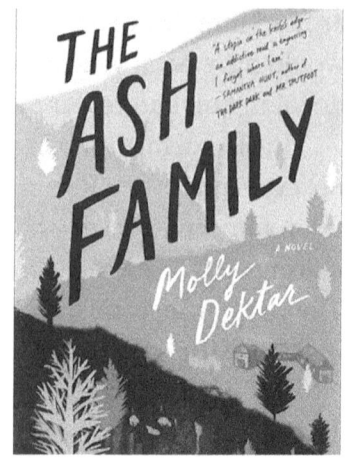

The novel opens in present day North Carolina on a road trip with nineteen year-old Berie and Bay, a new male acquaintance who is of an unknown age. The narrator, Berie proves to be predictably unreliable, which in the beginning makes for a slow reveal to get our bearings yet piques our interest with conflicting images. The intimacy with which she describes a person she just met, the adoration she bestows upon an unknown world, the disdain she feels for a seemingly unremarkable past, and the almost-lust she has for pain creates a disturbing character that keeps us turning pages. Once the novel is over one can re-read the first chapter and find every hint necessary to understand the prevalent themes, fulfilling one of the first rules of good fiction.

In the first bucolic paragraph, as the "first sun churned sideways through the trees, catching in the previous day's rain, which the wind now shook down from the Carolina silverbells, the beeches and the poplars," we receive a feast for the senses. Then we hear her idyllic voice again as she gazes at Bay and "the low sun lit up every strand of his hair, so that, as a result of its extreme disorder, it looked like a giant, bright halo." He has rescued her, she feels, and she makes him a consequential promise.

Throughout the novel there is not a flattering description of Bay, yet we continue to see his flaws through Berie's rose-colored glasses, perfectly characterizing her as an unreliable narrator to her own life. After Berie gets a splinter in her hand, she surrenders it to Bay for inspection and he inflicts pain, making it feel as if "he'd shoved a stake through my palm" as "a light went on in the house." Yet she doesn't complain, which becomes a metaphor for their entire relationship and for her inability to stand up for herself against outside authority. She's willing to give anybody authority over her, which as a character trait is maddening, but she's consistent to the end. Her attention to the light coming on in the house as her hand is driven with pain symbolizes her search for a Utopia regardless of personal pain or inconvenience.

It's not until the second chapter we realize that along with Berie, we have been picked up by a stranger at a bus stop and taken to the "Ash Family Farm", an intentional community compound, where Bay has said there is "no definite self" and that Berie can either "stay...three days or the rest of my life". By the time we find this out, it's too late for Berie and it's too late for us. She has been renamed Harmony and we are hooked until the end, vacillating between admiration for Dektar's linguistic skill and psychological insight, and the fear and frustration of Harmony's series of poor choices and dedication to an ideal regardless of consequence.

The people who find their way to the farm are drawn to protect the planet, reduce their carbon footprint, and stop harmful corporate practices. In exchange for a sense of purpose they learn to live off the land by natural means using crude but useful tools of antiquity, raising their own animals, and gardening for food. They conserve, preserve, and slaughter as instructed, sharing the work and the fruits thereof as a family, believing they live in Utopia. Yet their willingness to discard autonomy and individuality to follow their leader's narcissistic demands even to the level of violence and self-destruction is tantamount to mind control, thereby proving that utopia is a figment of the imagination. Dektar's knowledge of natural farming appears firsthand and spot on but so does her understanding of psychological warfare giving the reader education as well as entertainment.

Harmony's new life rules include "not being numbered", which translates to no doctors, no western medicine and sometimes unnecessary death. Although Bay, the farm's recruiter and most loyal follower, manipulates his personality to match the needs of the wayward souls he lures to the family, Harmony brings a willingness to be subdued and almost a desire to feel pain that is unnerving at times: "I'd always known what I wanted. I wanted to be pushed around, pushed onto the ground to break with a thud. Bay helped me put my own will back into it. I chose to be his passenger."

Each time Harmony reminisces or wrangles her old beliefs against the new rules put upon her by the Ash family, we garner hope that her past anger and misjudgment of her mother's intentions will subside and the harsh reality of her intentional community will reveal itself. Much like the character's sense of autonomy, our hopes are dashed by an immature teenager who misjudges and takes offense at all her mother's actions regardless of true fault while excusing every questionable action on the part of the Ash family. The perfect victim for a narcissistic agenda. Harmony seems to be sensory seeking, never reaching a plateau that proves too high or a standard set too low.

Ironically, it is our narrator's refusal to conform to mainstream norms of behavior and thought that sanctions her to conform to a life of punitive indoctrination. Equally as ironic is the bitter taste of dissatisfaction left on our palate by this character's refusal to grow internally while served on a platter of delicious metaphors, lyrical language, bucolic imagery, psychological insight, environmental stewardship and attention to detail. Dektar delivers a riveting feast.

**Misty Skaggs. *Planted by the Signs: Poems*. Athens, Oh.: Ohio University Press/Swallow Press, 2019. 112 pages. Softcover. $17.95.**

*Reviewed by Sylvia Woods*

*Planted by the Signs*, Misty Skaggs's first full-length collection of poetry, functions as a love letter to home, celebrating traditions of Appalachia and its "women who brought home the bacon and saved its grease." The collection is arranged according to the signs derived from the *Farmer's Almanac*, and while Skaggs depicts modern Appalachia as both beautiful and harsh, the women she knows are up to the challenge.

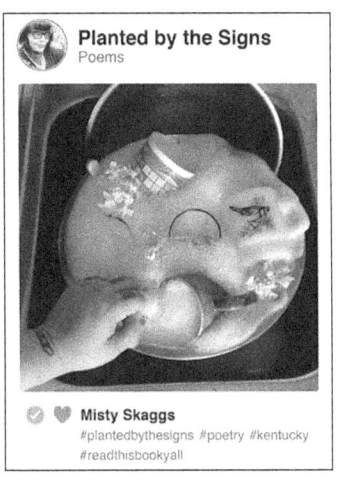

The signs are in the head for the first part of book with a poem set in the early morning. The images are vivid enough to feel the wet dew in the first poem set in the early morning. "Wet Dew," evokes solitude of living in a holler in Eastern Kentucky where all around there is sound. They are alone except for the sounds of nature at 5:30 a.m. The speaker sits quietly

*Except for the Cardinal*
*Screaming*
*"Wet dew! Wet Dew!"*
*one last time*
*before the light breaks*
*the whole holler.*

The writer's sense of belonging is evident; she claims these generations of her people belong to her in "Home Cemetery."

*We keep our dead*
*at the dead end*
*of a rutted gravel road.*
*Generations filed away*
*forever in staggered rows.*
*They belong to me.*

There are few positive descriptions of men, yet in "I'd Melt" the speaker confides she would want the kind of man who appreciates women who keep bacon grease, which is both tradition and ritual. She "longs for a love that holds up like cast iron." Other traditions held by her grandmother in "Oatmeal Communion" underscore the theme of women needing to protect each other. They warn about preachers and other people like Uncle Charlie who is in jail and might get out.

"Small Talk" explores the divide between the narrator and people who live in town. Even while characterizing country life as beautiful, Skaggs also that the experience can be hard to endure, not idyllic. The speaker feels disconnected listening to friends in town who dine on

*organic vegetables and vegan options...*
*My small talk is not spicy*
*like an authentic curry recipe.*
*It is salt and pepper.*

Her friends do not want to hear about the reality she endures taking care of a dying woman who "will never be ready to die." They don't want to hear of the agony, of "how her arm hurts and aches until she screams" and how the narrator "stays up all night" tending to her. Instead of harsh reality, the friends prefer details that entertain.

Life in the holler is not all birdsong and crickets. Like so many mountain women before her, she does what must be done, determined to persevere in spite of hardships. One of the most imagistic poems in the collection, "War Among the Cabbages," celebrates the battles inherent in gardening. This conversational poem addresses the reader and uses colloquialisms to describe her war with cutworms that "lurked deep. Mocking." She doesn't give up and digs into the dirt with spoon and sieve, "determined to slay/my solitary, slimy enemy."

"In the Call of the Creekbank" recalls the ever-present creeks and a wilderness where concrete is an obstacle. To Skaggs, the city is an unpleasant wilderness where "the buzz of hundreds of voices / took the place of the buzz / of honeybees in the hive." The city is a wilderness where "She balanced on tiptoes on her secondhand stiletto heels." The sidewalks are smooth, but she feels the urge to "make a break for the first creekbank she can find."

Women gather in "Breaking Beans" as an "assembly line." There is a sense of community and traditional labor division, of common purpose where women bond to complete the task. This poem ends with the recitation of the kinds of beans common in Eastern Kentucky gardens, further grounding sense of place.

"Momma and Mamaw and Them," one of the most powerful poems in the collection, explores a day in the life of three generations of women. The narrator listens as women tell stories and gossip when they break beans or shuck corn. They laugh and cuss as they do the chores to provide food for the family. There's clear love, mutual respect, and strength; "There was always something to do / and they women all lit in and went to it." The dialect in this poem is perfect. The metaphorical reference of women as hens suggests a closeness the speaker feels to her kin after a day of caring for children and livestock:

*Mommy and Mamaw and them*
*Pecked around like a whole pack*
*Of mother hens on the prowl.*

In "Breathing Ghosts" Skaggs uses the metaphor of dandelion fluff for herself. She's too deeply rooted in this place to ever be comfortable "on a rooftop garden." She's a "prodigy seed who will always land in the hills, in the boonies in Kentucky." She feels connected to the place, though the memory of ghosts is sometimes scary

*Because roots can get tangled*
*they can smother out*
*anything else*
*that dares*
*to grow close.*

Despite loneliness, Appalachian women don't fall apart. The speaker cares for her dying Great-Mamaw throughout the collection: "We are too busy holding it together to indulge in the pleasure of falling apart." Even in the face of death, they don't give up. If this collection is a love letter to Appalachia, it is also a celebration of its women.

**Jeff Mann & Julia Watts, eds.** *LGBTQ Fiction and Poetry from Appalachia.* **Morgantown, W. Va.: West Virginia University Press, 2019. 288 pages. Softcover. $29.99.**

*Reviewed by Melissa Helton*

If asked to describe yourself, what words would you choose? Most of our identities do not conflict with each other. Poet and environmentalist are pretty compatible. Mother and educator don't seem too antagonistic. What about queer and Appalachian? Trans and rural? *LGBTQ Fiction and Poetry from Appalachia,* edited by Jeff Mann and Julia Watts, crosses into spaces where "queer" and "Appalachian" can

be contentious or complementary, showing how queer lives play out in those spaces in all their beautiful and challenging intricacies. The introduction to the collection states the goal is to show that "queer" and "Appalachian" don't have to be mutually exclusive. The collection achieves that goal, but not without some noticeable missteps.

The collection is full of well-established names: Dorothy Allison, Silas House, Aaron Smith, Ann Pancake, and others, including the editors themselves. These writers are powerhouses in their craft and have proven themselves fearless in their LGBTQ writings and their commitment to the region. The pieces take readers into spaces they may or may not recognize. In "Saving," a short story by Carter Sickels, the main character visits Mamaw in the nursing home where she suffers dementia and hasn't seen her trans grandson since before his transition. The narrator of one of Savannah Sipple's poems shops at Walmart with Jesus. "Handling Dynamite," a short story by Watts, centers on a deep mine and a coal company town. Many pieces address the common struggle of *do-I-stay-or-do-I-go* that has fueled the Appalachian diaspora for generations, particularly for queer Appalachians. This, predictably, is often followed by the frequent desire—or requirement—to return "home."

While it is clear the editors made it a priority to gather diverse queer voices, the book would have benefitted from more examples of intersectionality in the LGBTQ+ community. The collection lacks an in-depth excavation of when queerness intersects with disability, Black identity (despite doris diosa davenport's poem "Black Lesbian Appalachian Identity," which is celebrated in the editors' note), parenthood, age, or violence. Bisexuality and pansexuality are absent in any meaningful way, which is often all-too-common in queer and straight spaces alike, making the anthology miss an opportunity to be inclusive of members of the LGBTQ+ community who identify as having a plural sexuality. Likewise, while there is work that features transgender characters, they are all trans men, and the collection is lacking a discussion of trans women, nonbinary folks, and those who identify as asexual or intersex.

That being said, I am stunned by this collection. So much of queer literature takes place elsewhere or in some amorphous non-place, and the pieces in this book weave together queer and Appalachian identities in ways in which it is tough to tell where one ends and the other begins. I dare say that may be the point. In Jonathan Corcoran's "The Rope Swing," queer desire unravels at the riverbank, a safe place where "an unthinkable touch of the hand, [is] rendered acceptable by the privacy of the forest." Nickole Brown's poem "To My Grandmother's Ghost, Flying with Me on a Plane" addresses the common conflict between queerness and religion when it asks what her grandmother Fanny thinks of the speaker's life. Additionally, the book offers a gem in its "Selected Bibliography of Same-Sex Desire in Appalachian Literature." It brings to our attention books and writers outside the collection by Davis Grubb, J.T. LeRoy, Lee Smith, and Karen Salyer McElmurray, among others. The bibliography is divided by genre and can be a helpful springboard for personal or scholarly reading lists, as well as a way to find representation in the broader literature missing from the selections in this collection.

*LGBTQ Fiction and Poetry from Appalachia* is a beautiful anthology showcasing some brilliant writers, and as "the first of its kind," as the introduction boasts, it certainly cannot include a representation of all queer Appalachian experiences—because as the book shows, there is no one experience. Our overlapping queer and Appalachian identities are as nuanced and individual as each creek, each road cut, each small and dusty church around us. This is a much-needed and timely anthology as more and more youths identify as something other than straight and cisgender, as more and more communities face decades-long population loss, as the rights and humanity of queer Americans are under attack on the local, state, and federal levels. As a queer person raising queer kids and teaching queer students in Appalachia, I am thrilled this collection is available. It fully embodies the advice Watts offers in the introduction: "Don't put an or where God puts an and."

We are a community of *and*. And that is beautiful. And we still have work to do to be inclusive and representative in our discussions of queerness. ■

# ALMOST HEAVEN,
## OR MIXED-RACE ROAD TRIP
## FOLLOWING THE FALL OF SAIGON

It was the song we'd sing
on those trips from Tennessee
to West Virginia

the massive Chrysler wagon
echoing with our voices
as soon as we'd cross the state

line in perfect five-part
non-harmony the road suddenly
dark from the steep-sided mountains

springing up like a headache
and because Mamaw forbade us
from taking the turnpike

on account of it being a death
trap Daddy steered us
on the squiggliest roads

the map could hold was it
Rand or McNally who drew
the red and black routes

the baby blue rivers and creeks
the dotted demarcations
that kept the counties apart

Fayette from Clay
Raleigh from Mingo
and me swooning

over towns that tasted
better than any candy
in the mouth Summerlee

and Sweetwood Mossy
and Lively and Hazy and
Naoma I could say Naoma

a thousand times over and never
tire of her music singing
the song meant we were

coming closer to the one place
on earth we were closest
to belonging two of us born there

one of us born and raised there
and two of us brought
there from a distant delta

our first home in this hemi-
sphere Mamaw's first encounter
with the enemy now

called kin and she loved
to hear us sing it would
make us sing it when we

arrived the car dark and dusty
from the miles and was that
a teardrop in her eye?

**ELIZABETH GORDON**

# CONTRIBUTORS

**Jenn Blair**'s work has been published or is forthcoming in the *James Dickey Review, Copper Nickel, The Chattahoochee Review, South Carolina Review, New South, Berkley Poetry Review, Tulane Review*, and *Pembroke Magazine*, among others. A graduate of Hollins University, she lives in Winterville, Georgia.

**Donna M. Crow,** a resident of Estill County, Kentucky is the third generation to live on her family farm. She writes fiction, creative nonfiction and poetry. Her work has appeared previously in *Appalachian Heritage, Still: The Journal, Now and Then, The Minnetonka Review, The Louisville Review, Blue Lyra Review,* and other publications. She received her MFA in Creative Nonfiction from Spalding University.

Originally from West Virginia, **Jae Dyche** holds an MFA in Creative Writing from the University of Maryland and is entering the PhD in Rhetorics, Communication, and Information Design at Clemson University. She lives in the Virginian Blue Ridge and works at a Fine and Performing Arts high school in Manassas, Virginia. Her work most recently appears in *Tule Review, Harpur Palate, Sheila-Na-Gig* online, and *Triggerfish Critical Review.*

**Robert Gipe** won the 2015 Weatherford Award for outstanding Appalachian novel for his first novel *Trampoline*. His second novel is Weedeater (2018). Both novels were published by Ohio University Press. From 1997 to 2018, Gipe directed the Southeast Kentucky Community & Technical College Appalachian Program in Harlan. He is a producer of the *Higher Ground* community performance series and resides in Harlan County, Kentucky.

Raised in southern Appalachia, **Elizabeth Gordon** is a Vietnamese-American poet and playwright whose work has appeared in numerous anthologies and journals including *CutThroat, Slant, Appalachian Life,* and *New Millennium Writing*s, among others. A Pushcart Prize nominee and recipient of the Tennessee Arts Commission's Literature

Fellowship in Poetry, she holds an MFA from Brown University and divides her time between Massachusetts and coastal North Carolina.

**Rebecca Hazelwood** holds an MFA in Creative Writing from Georgia College and a PhD in English/Creative Writing from the University of Louisiana at Lafayette. She also runs the poetry blog *Structure and Style*. Her essays have appeared in *Guernica, Anthropoid, Hobart, PANK, Still: The Journal*, and *December*, where she was a finalist for the Curt Johnson Prose Award in Nonfiction.

**Melissa Helton** is Associate Professor of English at Southeast Kentucky Community and Technical College. Originally from the Great Lakes region, she has called southeast Kentucky home since 2010. Her poetry, nonfiction, and photography have appeared in *Anthology of Appalachian Writers, Still: The Journal, Pine Mountain Sand and Gravel*, and more. Her chapbook *Inertia: A Study* was published in 2016.

**Bethany Holmstrom** is an Associate Professor of English at LaGuardia Community College, City University of New York. Originally from Bedford County, Virginia, she now resides in Brooklyn and is pursuing her MFA at City College, CUNY.

**Mary Alice Hostetter**'s writing has appeared in the *New York Times, Gettysburg Review, Prime Number, Hippocampus, storySouth, The Common*, and previously in *Appalachian Heritage*. She lives with her wife in Charlottesville, Virginia.

**Lisa M. Kendrick** lives in the heart of Norfolk, Virginia with her twin daughters. She has been teaching high school English for twenty-five years; publishes a high school literary magazine; writes curriculum, young adult fiction, and poetry; and performs spoken word in her spare time. Her work has most recently been published in *Soundings, Perspectives, Sister Stories, Red Weather, Moonstone Press*, and *River River*.

**Emily Masters** is a graduate of Berea College and serves as book reviews editor for *Appalachian Review*. She is from Monteagle, Tennessee, where she lives on a farm with her family. Her work has been published in *Still: The Journal* and *The Pikeville Review*.

**L. Renée** is a poet from Columbus, Ohio. She is a second-year MFA candidate at Indiana University, where she serves as Nonfiction Editor of the Indiana Review and Associate Director of the Indiana University Writers' Conference. Her work has been supported by Fine Arts Work Center in Provincetown, Kenyon Review Writers Workshop and Minnesota Northwoods Writers Conference. Her poems have been published or are forthcoming in *Tin House Online, Poet Lore, Southern Humanities Review,* and *New Limestone Review.*

**Savannah Sipple** is the author of *WWJD and Other Poems.* Her writing has been published in *Southern Cultures, Split This Rock, Salon, Appalachian Heritage, Waxwing,* and other places. The recipient of grants from the Money for Women/Barbara Deming Memorial Fund and the Kentucky Foundation for Women, she serves as an Assistant Professor of English at Bluegrass Community and Technical College. She resides in Lexington, Kentucky, with her wife, Ashley.

**Alison Terjek** is a poet currently living in Northwest Connecticut. She served 2017-2019 as a Service to Improve Community Health (STICH) AmeriCorps Member. Her work has been published recently in *Causeway Lit, Northern New England Review, The Adirondack Review,* and *Burningword Literary Journal.* She is most inspired by her time outdoors in rural New England, life's joy and challenges, and her work in the community.

**Raymond Thompson Jr.** is a freelance photographer and multimedia producer based in Morgantown, West Virginia. He works as a Multimedia Producer at West Virginia University while pursing an MFA in photography from the institution. He received his Masters degree from the University of Texas at Austin in journalism and graduated from the University of Mary Washington with a B.A. in American Studies. He has worked as a freelance photographer for the *New York Times, The Intercept,* NBC News, *ProPublica,* WBEZ, Google, Merrell, and the Associated Press.

**Vanessa Van Besien** is an MFA candidate in Fiction at the University of New Hampshire. Her work has been nominated for a Pushcart Prize. Most recently, she won the Thomas Williams Memorial Award for Excellence in Fiction. She lives in Dover, New Hampshire with her cat, Stevens, teaches First-Year Writing, bartends, and manages to find the time to play Dungeons and Dragons three nights a week.

**Frank X Walker** is the author of eight collections of poetry, including *Turn Me Loose: The Unghosting of Medgar Evers*, winner of the 2014 NAACP Image Award for Poetry and *Buffalo Dance: The Journey of York*, winner of the 2004 Lillian Smith Book Award. The recipient of a 2005 Lannan Literary Fellowship, Walker is Professor of English and African American and Africana Studies at the University of Kentucky.

**Sylvia Woods**, a native of Kentucky, is a former English teacher who lives in Oak Ridge, Tennessee. Her work has appeared in many anthologies and literary journals, including *Appalachian Heritage, Motif,* and *The Southern Poetry Anthology*. She is working on a collection of poems about language.

www.ingramcontent.com/pod-product-compliance
Lightning Source LLC
Chambersburg PA
CBHW070558180626
46817CB00005B/1895